Brian (Hutch) Hutchinson: acrobat, musician (sax/clarinet), civil servant, special advisor to cabinet minister, music business executive, theatrical agent, recording studio partner, record factory managing director, director Brixton Business Centre/Brixton City Challenge, general manager on secondment with the Diana, Princess of Wales Memorial Fund, patron Macmillan Academy Teesside, independent assessor for commissioner for (ministerial) public appointments, corporate affairs director Allied Zurich Plc, chair UK trustees International Fund for Animal Welfare, former trustee National Centre for Circus Arts.

In memory of Dr Deborah (Rebba) Hutchinson (nee Main), my love of 55 years: consultant psychiatrist/psychotherapist, mother of Sophie, George and Eleanor, grandmother to Molly, Clara, Tom, Finbarr, Wilfred and Margot, whom sadly she never knew.

Brian Hutchinson

WAITING IN THE WINGS

AUSTIN MACAULEY PUBLISHERS™

LONDON • CAMBRIDGE • NEW YORK • SHARJAH

A CIP catalogue record for this title is available from the British Library.

ISBN 9781528983761 (Paperback)
ISBN 9781528984447 (ePub e-book)

www.austinmacauley.com

First Published (2020)
Austin Macauley Publishers Ltd
25 Canada Square
Canary Wharf
London
E14 5LQ

To my extended family and friends who supported me in my efforts to be published. Also to Hester Vazey whose help in improving my text was invaluable.

Chapter 1

The result of being born in the middle of a war, brought up as the only male in a female household, with a father away fighting the Germans and Italians in North Africa meant that I was thoroughly over-indulged.

My mother, grandmother and I lived in a small, dark flat in Fulham. My first memories of the flat are of a vast, dark place with a few light and warm places. The open coal fires (I even had one in my bedroom) – were such a comfort.

I began life on St Andrew's day 1941, Winston Churchill's birthday and six days before the Japanese attack on Pearl Harbour. My grandmother told me many times how foggy it was and, how a friend of hers who lived at Parsons Green walked through the fog from the maternity home to bring the news of my birth. Listening to her in later years as she recalled the events, it set in my mind just how small the world seemed in those days before instant communications were at everybody's fingertips.

I suppose I just have 'memory bytes' of those times. The tail of a German V1 fell in our back yard. As a small boy in my cot, I was told that it was a dustbin lid falling down and that everything was alright. Everything was always alright: I was cushioned from the terrors of war by my mother and grandmother and I feel strangely guilty even today when I think of the horrors others were going through, whilst I lived in my own safe world, not knowing until much later in life just how awful things were elsewhere.

We lived opposite a Threshers bottling warehouse and the Luftwaffe were always dropping incendiary bombs on the building. The bottles, heated by the fires, used to pop their corks or explode. I can still hear the sound in my mind's 'ear' today.

As I grew older, my capacity to be looked after by women increased. The two ladies in the upstairs flat, along with Mother and Grandmother, used to lean over my cot during bombing raids to protect me. God knows what would have resulted in a direct hit! We rarely used the air-raid shelters although one was built in the road directly opposite our flat. I think people felt more vulnerable all grouped together in what might quite easily become a concrete tomb.

My mother worked some of the time as a film extra. She and her friend Stella Stafford, whose husband was away in the RAF; still show up in crowd scenes in many of the old wartime movies shown on TV today, such as *This Happy Breed*, *The Wicked Lady* and *Spring in Park Lane* starring Anna Negal.

I have early memories of my mother leaving the flat at 5 am to get to Elstree, Pinewood or Teddington and not getting home until late at night. Sometimes she was delayed by the bombing raids or disrupted train and trolleybus services. But life went on.

Being left in the care of my grandmother was a treat for me. Not that my mother was anything less than indulgent, but Grandmother seemed calmer. My mother was constantly concerned, although I did not know it, about my father. I learned later on that he was a paratrooper and trained the SAS to drop behind enemy lines. More of him later. My grandmother, however, had been widowed in 1929 after bringing seven children into the world. Six of them survived so I had three uncles and two aunts, my mother being the third and youngest girl. Grandmother had a worldly calm about her and it was impossible, even when I was a grown man, not to feel calm whenever she was about.

From 1941 through to the end of the war in 1945, we moved away from London several times to avoid the bombing. It was never very successful. Maybe our movements were personally known to Herr Hitler! We moved to Birmingham to stay with my uncle Ted. And then the Luftwaffe increased their bombing of the Midlands. We moved to Bournemouth, where my Mother's elder sister Peggy's wealthy in-laws owned a huge house on Alum Chime. It was like a wonderland for me. Red squirrels in the pine trees. Cousin Anthony, who was six weeks older than me, had a pedal car. There was a real Daimler in the garage which smelt of leather and polish. And in Bournemouth there seemed no shortages of the luxuries of life, such as chocolate cake, sweets and ice cream.

My maternal grandmother, Sophia Jane Phillips

I was never sure whether it was the Germans who used to bring our frequent stays to an end. Maybe it was something more mundane, that we were the poor side of the family and could only be tolerated for short periods of time.

It is difficult to remember clearly the images of very young childhood. I recall sitting on the kitchen floor whilst a man in soldiers' uniform hammered tacks into the lino' on the floor to hold it down. I had always assumed it was my father, but the timing was wrong as he did not see me until I was four years old. Most likely it was my uncle Frank who was not posted overseas until later in the war.

I first met my father in Bournemouth. My mother, grandmother and I were again staying with my aunt's in-laws at Dene Edge. Someone said there was a soldier coming down the road towards the house. The road was a cul-de-sac and Dene Edge was the last house so that it faced right up the road. I remember running towards the soldier and being overtaken by my cousin Anthony. Alas, it was not my Dad but his: my Uncle Neville was back from the war with gifts for his family. My disappointment was assuaged some days later when my dad actually turned up – back from Italy where he had been fighting when Germany finally gave in. He was to be stationed in the UK until demobbed from the Army. He was strikingly good looking, strong, slim and suntanned from his time in Italy. I had no way of recognising him on first meeting as I had no memory of the many photographs I'd been shown. I gradually got to know him at weekends when he came home on leave. I remember his uniform, especially his red paratroopers' beret and his Crown Badge above his three Sergeant's stripes. Suddenly the Fulham flat smelled different: Dad smoked 60 John Players a day. My mother did not seem to be around so much, but when she was, she seemed more relaxed and happier with life. I remember clearly being allowed into my parents' bed in the mornings. Dad had an army watch with a luminous face which he would hold under the bedclothes so I could see it magically glow.

My dad finally left the Army in 1945. His demob suit was double-breasted and angular, but he looked very good in it. He was still extremely fit even though he had been shot through the back during his time in Africa. A professional acrobat by background, my father had been able to keep up his training during his four years away as a physical training instructor in the Army. He was soon taking me to the Express Dairy café on the Charing Cross Road where variety artistes and their agents still met on Saturday mornings to fix the next week's engagements in some awful provincial theatre. Dad had come to an agreement with an old acrobatic acquaintance, Victor Scott, to form a new troupe to be called the Rapid Four. My mother, who was a dancer when she and Dad met, decided not to work in the troupe, but instead to stay at home and look after me. Even at my young age I realised that this caused some tension in their relationship.

Mother felt that moving around the UK – a different town and theatre every week – was no way to bring up her only child. However, as things settled down post-war, life developed a definite pattern in the Hutchinson household.

Chapter 2

There were two periods in the year when my father's troupe would be resident for more than a week or so; they were the Summer Season and the Pantomime Season. The rest of the year he would be touring the provinces, the Number 1 and Number 2 theatres that every town and city boasted. So my young life was divided between the months of the year when I hardly ever saw him and those wonderful months when my mother and I (sometimes Grandmother too) spent my school holidays in whichever town he was resident. As a child I knew Blackpool, Brighton, Clacton, Great Yarmouth, Morecambe, Eastbourne and Bournemouth, where he was in Summer Season, like the back of my hand. Usually in Summer Season we would rent a cottage or small flat, so it was just like moving house for a three-month period. For Pantomime Season we would go into theatrical 'digs' in the provinces. So Christmas Day became an event wherever we were and I used to enjoy traveling on the train with my mother to wherever he was working.

My father's birthday in Clacton. He's standing Centre, my mother
to his right and grandmother to his left, and me aged 6.

My first real memory of Summer Season was Clacton on
Sea. The Rapid Four was in a show at the Pier Theatre and we
rented a house at the back of the town. Its garden overlooked
the local farm where the wheat was golden brown and the
weather was fantastic. This was where I made my first
tentative step or leap into show business. Dad and members
of the act used to rehearse most mornings in the week for an
hour or so, perfecting new acrobatic tricks. Usually he would
make arrangements with the stage manager to use the stage
for this unless the weather was good and there was some grass
or a good beach nearby. Acrobats, good ones that is, have
always enjoyed 'showing off'. But whereas in the theatre,
people expect to see the clever tricks and can be quite blasé
about it, in ordinary surroundings, the beach or park, a good
row of flip-flaps neatly finished with a double somersault can
attract a big crowd. At the entrance to Clacton pier was
enough flat space to rehearse and one morning Dad got busy.
Once the expertly delivered acrobatic tricks had gathered a

large crowd it was my turn. I must have been five years old at the time and fairly skinny. Three acrobats made a 'three high' pyramid and then I was hauled, from hand to hand, to the top to make 'four high'. It would have been easy to become terrified except that the strength and firmness of these very strong men made me feel that nothing could go wrong. In fact throughout my young life I truly believed that my father could achieve anything. I remember looking down from the top of the pyramid at the crowd and seeing other members of the act taking the hat round.

It was this event, more than any, that made me certain I wanted to be the world's greatest acrobat when I grew up. Time would tell whether this was to be.

Chapter 3

In 1946, when I was just 5 years old, I started to attend All Saints' School in Fulham High Street. My lasting memory is of the first morning in a large class of 40. I didn't like it a bit. Our teacher was constantly flustered and overwhelmed so that it was difficult to attract her attention. One embarrassing morning, after desperately trying to get her attention, I could wait no longer and wet myself. God, I can still feel the embarrassment as I was sent home to change! Early school days were very trying as I was unfamiliar with the surroundings and the people. The smell of cod liver oil tablets, sour milk and sweaty feet still lingers in my mind today.

The Headmaster of All Saints was Mr Frisby and he had taught my Uncle Vernon at the school too. Vernon was my Grandmother's youngest and favourite son. An admirable, hard-working school boy who also sang in the All Saint's Church choir. Frisby thought he was great and I thought I would never be able to live up to his reputation. I guess I just struggled my way through the early primary school years. I made friends and got used to the daily routine. My best friend was a dark, tough boy called Tony Baker. His father was a sea captain and never at home (that was always the excuse his mother gave). Tony Baker and his mother lived in Hurlingham Road in two rooms on the first floor. His uncle's family lived down stairs and his uncle was an engineer. No ordinary engineer as he used to make the most fantastic model steam engines which you could ride on. Models of traction engines which were powerful enough to pull a trailer of children round the garden. I loved visiting just to see and smell these working models.

My Uncle Vernon had an only daughter, Wendy, who went to a 'posh' private school in Munster Road run by a music teacher called Miss James. Wendy was an excellent young pianist and a brilliant sight reader, something to this day I have never accomplished. Miss James gave piano lessons at her home in the evenings, so my parents thought I should play the piano too. I took to it quite easily although my sight reading to this day is poor. This musical endeavour helped me to become more popular at school, at least with the staff. Many of my class mates thought it was cissy to play the piano, and I was teased and bullied for a while. I was always asked to play in school concerts and, at the age of six years, was quite confident, no nerves. This was to prove an unbearable burden for me in my teens when I became self-conscious and terrified of performing solo in public – more of which later.

I was not very quick at school: my handwriting was terrible and my spelling even worse. This, however, all changed when Mr Frisby retired and Mr Crosby, a genial and very practical Yorkshire man, took over as Head. Mr Crosby was very keen on handwriting, italic copperplate handwriting with proper italic nibs. I had never taken to anything so quickly in my short life and soon became the star pupil. I was asked to write notices for the teachers' notice board and my confidence grew. Along with this confidence my other work improved too and in 1948 I was given the greatest accolade All Saints' could offer I was made Bell Boy. The school faced onto Fulham High Street where the double front door provided access for the teaching staff, visitors and, the most important visitor of all, the School Inspector. The front door bell was the old-fashioned type: a handle connected to a wire connected to a real brass bell suspended on a coiled spring. When a visitor rang this bell, the Bell Boy was expected to leave whatever lesson or task he was involved in and run to answer the door. This privileged position was envied by the children and resented by many of the teachers who had to ignore the little upstart rushing from class in the middle of a lesson. Upon answering the bell, I enquired who the visitor wished to see and then escorted the person to, usually, the headmaster. It meant that I met every VIP who visited the school, saw the Headmaster frequently and kept up-to-date with all the gossip regarding whose parents had been summoned in for a ticking-off about little Ann or Jimmy's behaviour. I think it was my time as Bell Boy which made me ambitious later on to be close to the seat of power in my adult working life.

I had one real difficulty at primary (and later secondary) school. I was lousy at PE. Me, with a father who rightly claimed to be 'Britain's Greatest Acrobat', I couldn't vault a horse, climb a rope or win a fight in the playground. It was awful! I was so full of admiration for my dad that I hid in his shadow. My mother was determined that I should not follow in father's mega leaps and inside I was very angry about this. What made matters worse was that Dad was recruiting young school leavers as apprentices and, when the act was in London, they lived with us in the flat. They were great fun to have around, but here was my father teaching his marvellous tricks to someone else's children. They were all the things I wasn't, strong, athletic and free. Whenever I was on school holidays, I nagged Dad to teach me. Initially he tried, but my mother put a lot of pressure on him so, for a bit of peace, he gave up.

Chapter 4

During the years between 1945 and 1952 several events stand out in my memory. The 1947 winter when we had 8 feet snow drifts in our small back yard. To keep warm, we had open coal fires and the coal for these was in the cellar. As I grew up and became stronger it was my job to bring buckets of coal up from the cellar. I loved the cellar. It smelt damp and musty and, in the areas not used for coal, the people in the upstairs flats stored unwanted belongings, such as old clocks and radios which I asked for and was given. I mended many of these and was even able to wire up an old headphone to the back of a radio and use it as a microphone. I think I gave my family a big shock by turning the radio on and hiding under the bed with my home-made microphone. "This is a request for Jean Hutchinson of Buer Road Fulham from her husband, the world-famous acrobat Johnny Hutch, who is currently appearing at the London Palladium." Looking back, I was lucky not to have electrocuted myself as the earphone gave a tingling sensation when my lips touched the metal part!

When my mother went off to join Dad for the odd week or two in the provinces, my grandmother sometimes took me out on Friday evenings. We would walk over Putney Bridge and get on an LCC River Bus at Putney Pier. This would take us to Charing Cross Pier where we would get off and walk up to Lyons Corner House in Coventry Street. Here we would go into the Egg and Bacon Restaurant for supper and then onto a News Theatre. There were a dozen or so of these small cinemas in the West End where you could see the latest British Movitone or Pathe News and six cartoons (Loony Tunes with Bugs Bunny, Tweety and Sylvestor and MGM's

Tom and Gerry, not to mention the Walt Disney favourites) all for one shilling and three pence (1/3d). Having done this, we would then walk through to the Kingsway Tram Subway where a number 35 tram would take us through the tunnel, very exciting, dark with moony flashes of electricity, out onto the Embankment and over Westminster Bridge to the Elephant and Castle. Here we would change onto a number 4 tram to Wimbledon from where we would board a 93 bus to Putney Bridge Station (in Fulham) and walk home.

The old London trams were fascinating: many of them, destined for the scrap yard in the 1930s, were saved by the War. It was like riding in a time-warp. At night they were all lit up like Christmas Trees and when they crossed a section gap there would be a moment of darkness followed by a flash of blue light before the interior light came on again.

The trams had a great feeling of permanence about them with their rails in the middle of the road; they ran all day and all through the night. Today, if I want to recapture those times, I have on video a copy of 'The Elephant Will Never Forget' made by British Transport Films in 1952. It is a classic of its time and a much better way of reliving the past than me trying to capture the atmosphere in words.

I vividly remember the Festival of Britain in 1951, a national fair and exhibition which celebrated the inventiveness of British scientists and technologists. The Dome of Discovery and Skylon were particular highlights. I visited the exhibition many times during the year and still have my commemorative five-shilling piece as a reminder. I remember gluing myself to the radio for the closing ceremony and shedding a tear when they played Land of Hope and Glory. It was the end of an era for me. The trams finally vanished from London's streets in 1952 and I still remember the feeling of anger I had as a small boy. Why take away something so permanent, spoil my Friday treat with no means of my registering a small objection? The era really ended for me when, in 1953, I moved from All Saints Primary to Henry Compton Secondary School a mile or so up the Fulham Palace Road.

Chapter 5

'A small pea in a large pod' largely captures how I felt on the move to Senior School. Henry Compton Secondary School was one of the first comprehensives to be established in London. It was formed by amalgamating Fulham Central with Kingswood Road Secondary Modern. With a combined role of 2,000 boys it was a vast school.

I had failed my 11 plus, so the old grammar schools were not available to me. Anyway, I was in Form 1A of an eight-form entry. There were 43 of us in the class and our form master had great difficulty controlling so many boys. However, we were the cream of the intake unlike the other end – Form 1H, where most of the boys could neither read nor write! It was a truly 'comprehensive' intake.

That first term at Henry Compton was a nightmare for me and in the end of term tests I came 41st out of 43. It was such an awful shock that I can remember to this day the feeling of hopelessness. I couldn't sleep and just didn't know what to do. Fortunately, I was not relegated to a lower form in the spring term and, by some miracle and lots of extra hard work, I came 2nd in the end of spring term exams. By this time my self-confidence had returned and I was starting to get involved in school life.

Meanwhile my father had bought me a second hand clarinet from Billy Amstell in Wardour Street, and I was to have lessons from a professional player. Ivor Mariants and Eric Guilder had just started the Central School of Dance Music and this is where I was to go every Saturday morning for lessons with Basil (Nick) Tchykov, a splendid classical player. He did not think much of the instrument that Billy

Amstel sold my dad, however he persevered with me and I became a tolerably proficient player in a fairly short time.

This put me in a favourable light at Henry Compton, where the music master was putting together the school's first orchestra. His name was George Hutchinson and he hailed from Sunderland. He was a good double bass player and played professionally with the Southern Philharmonic but he was an impatient man not ideally suited to teaching: "Strike me pink boy, what are you doing now?!" was an all too familiar phrase. In any case, he formed the school orchestra (to play popular classics) in which I became a star player. However, a musical conflict was to emerge at the school: classics versus jazz.

It was the early 1950s and a new friend, Peter Roberts, had just been given a drum kit for his birthday. Peter also had one of the early Gerry Mulligan Chet Baker West Coast Jazz albums, not bad for a 12-year-old. When he first played it to me, I was totally hooked and have remained so ever since. Peter's drum kit was set up in his bedroom where he would play along with the record for hours. We then heard Art Blakey and got hold of a recording of *Blues March*. The Roberts' neighbours must have been the most tolerant people in Putney. It's interesting how Blakey grabbed us because in more recent times his influence on young jazz players such as Wynton Marsalis was immense. Even after his death, Art Blakey is amazingly influential. We had two music masters, Hutchinson, who I've mentioned and Mr Kitchen I have not. He was a very good pub pianist with a great love for traditional jazz. So, we formed a school jazz band: me on clarinet and alto sax, Peter Roberts on drums, David Pibworth (who now works for the UN) on trumpet and Atkins on double bass. One end of term open evening and art exhibition the orchestra performed some classics which were well received.

Then, as a surprise, several of us came back on as the Jazz Band and brought the house down. It was great for us but the Classical Mr Hutchinson never forgave us for this public up-staging.

Another amusing incident happened at the same event but to do with the art exhibition. Henry Compton's Head of Art was Mr Eustace, a bohemian painter: red beard, green tweed jacket, bright yellow and red tie, and very approachable. Form 1A had the whole of Monday afternoon as an art period. The art room was an add-on to the main building and was built on the roof with an outside terrace. With great views over south west London, it was a haven away from the normal pressures of school life. A lot of chatter took place during Monday afternoon and much of it was about 'Journey into Space' which was broadcast on Monday evenings by the BBC Light Programme. Produced by Charles Chiltern and featuring David Kossof and a young David Jacobs, it still rates in my memory as one of the best and most gripping science-fiction productions ever. Done right, radio drama can be the best. However, I digress. Eustace was a great and talented art master, so quite naturally the school produced some good work. This work was displayed at the musical end-of-term open evening where, prior to the concert, David Pibworth and I were on duty to show parents and guests around. An extraordinarily beautiful young woman arrived and was greeted by Pibworth and me. Towards the end of the evening Mr Eustace came to where we were standing. "Wonderful bit of crumpet over there, Sir" said Dave. To which Eustace replied "Pibworth, that is my wife!" Eustace was no spring chicken and his reputation went up one hundred-fold with the lads in 1A after that.

I progressed through my secondary school years fairly smoothly and on course to take 10 GCE's. As my world broadened, I became less keen on taking a career in the entertainment business. I liked my evenings and weekends, enjoying the social side of life. My parents' social world was very narrow and I put much of this down to the anti-social hours they worked. When they were working, most of the population was socialising.

As a teenager, I still joined my parents wherever they were based for the Summer and Pantomime Seasons during my school holidays. On some occasions I would work in the act when one of the team was injured or sick. I quite enjoyed this although it made me very nervous. My father had been allowed to teach me a few tricks; my best was a 'tinska' which is an Arab cartwheel. I was very good at them and performed a few variations: Tinska Mical (on the spot), Tinska turns (one handed and two handed) and Tinskas round. Whilst these tricks were not dangerous, they looked impressive and went down well with audiences. However, this was just an interlude for me and I was always glad to get back to my friends in London.

Just before my 16th birthday in 1957, I vividly remember facing a big decision. On a number 14 bus with my mother en route to the West End to buy me a jacket, out of the blue she asked me if I would like to leave school and join my father's acrobatic act the Volants who were off to Southern Africa to work with Boswell's Circus for a year. What a shock! I said I would like to think about it for a day or two. What would happen if I opted not to go? I asked. Could I stay with my grandmother in the Fulham flat and take my GCEs? My mother was adamant that if I stayed then she would stay too. If I agreed to go, then we would all go, Grandmother too. Couldn't I live with the Roberts family for a year, I asked? No, she was not happy with that either.

I was uncertain of my own wishes and very concerned that if I did not go then the family would be broken up. I really did not want to see my parents living apart for such a long period and I did not relish living with my mother's depression during that time. In the end I opted to take advice from my Headmaster. Mr White was a tough character but very fair and worldly. To my immense surprise he advised me to go saying that travel broadened the mind, I could always sit the GCE's later and an opportunity to visit Africa might only come once in a lifetime. I therefore told my relieved parents that I would join them.

There was a lot to organise before departing for South Africa. Firstly, I needed a license from Bow Street Magistrates' Court to allow an underage person to perform abroad, followed by medical checks every three months whilst we were away to enable renewal of the license. My father had to deposit £400 with the Court as a surety.

There were many other things to organise as well in that November of 1956: saying goodbye, letting the flat, buying lightweight clothes. Leaving school and all my friends, time just flew by. My friend Peter Roberts and his dad came to Waterloo on a foggy November morning to see us off on the boat train to Southampton. In those days the train went right on to the quayside, and we were soon being allocated our cabins on the SS Winchester Castle, one of the older ships of the Union Castle Line.

Chapter 6

The voyage marked the beginning of my personal baptism of fire into the acrobatics world. I was surrounded by acrobats and had just two weeks to become one myself! Once the ship got underway, we got to know our future compatriots also traveling to join Boswells Circus at Cape Town. Trevor Bale was the lion tamer and, with his family, also juggled, rode unicycles and put his precocious 15-year-old daughter Gloria on the high trapeze. We were to find out later that Trevor hated lions and was really terrified before each performance.

Then there were the Trio Chromatique, father, mother and large daughter Carol. Mum and Dad played the accordion and Carol the Xylophone. They dressed up in clothes covered in small mirrors to reflect the spot lights.

Big Tiflute, me in the middle. Johannesburg Xmas 1957

Then there was us. My mother, father and grandmother. Then the four acrobat employees Carol Ryan, Peter Morressey, Colin Stewart (my cousin), and Bernard Bryan.

There were also other artists travelling to South Africa on board. The Dagenham Girl Pipers were joining the rival Wilkie's Circus. There were also twelve ice skaters going to join the Ice Show in Johannesburg. Cousin Colin could not believe his luck!

A two-week sea journey to Cape Town sounds great fun, but it does get more than a little boring 'locked up' with the same people for a length of time. There were dances though, and we put on a show in which I played the clarinet. There was the crossing the Equator ceremony, a drenching in flour/water paste then thrown fully clothed into the ship's swimming pool.

We visited Madeira for eight hours where we were taken ashore by lighters as the Winchester Castle was too big to be berthed. I distinctly remember a very hairy return to the ship as there were enormous waves. My grandmother was scooped up by three big sailors and transferred from the small lighter to the ship. She was 76 years old and had never left the UK prior to this trip. What a baptism of fire!

On circus site L-R: Jean Hutch (my mum), Carol Ryan, Peter Morressey, Johnny Hutch (my dad), me, Colin Stewart (my cousin), and Bernard Bryan

Chapter 7

When we arrived at Cape Town the circus tent was already pitched on the South Shore. Boswells had booked us all into the Castle Hotel, which was pretty third-rate, but clean, at least. Soon after settling in, there was music rehearsal – not the usual circus line-up as the musical director Henri Samethini was Dutch Indonesian and had learnt jazz improvisation from American musicians in Japanese prison camps during the Second World War. He played the Hammond Organ and had an excellent brass player and drummer on the permanent staff. When the circus hit the large towns and cities the line-up was augmented, but more of this later.

The circus opening night came and went very smoothly. We played for two weeks in Cape Town and I was getting used to being an acrobat, although I still only performed Tinskas in their various forms. We did a fair bit of sightseeing, up Table Mountain and visiting the many excellent beaches. I missed my London friends but there was so much to do, so no time yet for regret. Towards the end of the second week we went to view the train which, in one form or another, was to be our travelling home for the next 12 months and 75,000 miles of Southern Africa. Three old style, open balconied, wooden carriages just like those used in Cowboy Westerns, which would be coupled either directly behind the locomotive or at the very rear of the train behind the goods wagons carrying the circus animals. Only short night journeys to begin with, we were told. We were to occupy one half of a carriage with exclusive use of a toilet and balcony. It was all very exciting to begin with. Our first overnight journey was from Cape Town to Paarl. We made ourselves at home on the train, moving into our half carriage during the day before the final Cape Town performance. After the show that night we returned to the train where I made an excellent spaghetti supper on the new double burner Primus stove we had purchased along with canvas water carriers (which we hung outside on the balcony to cool the water by evaporation). We went to bed around 1 am and I vaguely remember feeling movement in my sleep and distant railway noises. I awoke at 9 am to find we were in a siding at Paarl Station, plugged into the local electricity with the tent visible about a quarter of a mile away. It was not the same tent as we had in Cape Town. Boswells had two tents which they 'leapfrogged' on one-night stands. The tents were the only equipment not to travel by rail. Each tent had its own crew who travelled on a day ahead so that wherever and whenever we arrived in a town the tent was already erected. It was very well managed and we hardly missed a performance during the whole tour.

My Dad paid me £10 per week for tumbling in the act, plus my board and lodgings. He put £5 of that into a savings account, leaving me with a fiver; but it went a long way – twenty okay Bazaar ciggies, for example, cost two and sixpence (12.1/2p). I tried smoking but, luckily for me, hated it and soon gave up.

One evening before one of the Stellenbosch shows, I noticed Stanley Boswell talking to my Dad, who was looking and pointing in my direction. He gesticulated for me to join them. Mr Stanley (we had strict instructions to be polite to the management) was telling Dad that they augmented the circus band when standing in larger towns. He'd heard that I played sax and clarinet and asked whether I would join the band for £5 a week! I was thrilled as the Musical Director – Henri Samethini – was a great jazz player and as I previously mentioned as a Javan national he had been interned by the Japanese with a whole unit of American jazz musicians during the Second World War, and they had built a keyboard and taught him the rudiments of jazz.

As I only performed in one of the two acrobatic spots we did in the circus, I was available to play in the band for most of the performances. We wore sort of military band costumes on the bandstand and I wore a sailor's costume in the Volants acrobatic act. We also underdressed in very tight jock-straps for the acrobatics, so to make a quick change, I wore my jock-strap on the bandstand, to the great hilarity of the other players – you can imagine the comments: good for hitting the high notes!

The band had a very good trumpet player, Stan, who had broadcast on SABC (South African Broadcasting Company). He was a good-looking man with a very dark complexion and we became friends. Half way through the year's tour he was reclassified non-white and had to move his permanent address from a whites-only area to a coloured area. The apartheid regime was not only obscene, it was completely barmy! He could play on the bandstand with us, but was not allowed in the same hotels or restaurants.

Life on the train was new and engaging. We had no travel worries and no involvement in erecting and dismantling the tent: this was all done by white management and non-white labour. Boswells employed around 70 'boys' to set up and take down the tents.

We worked our way up the country towards Johannesburg where we were based for three weeks over the Christmas period 1957/8. The Cape, Transvaal, Orange Free State: it was all very new and unexpected. In some towns it was obvious that the Afrikaners hated the English. We quickly learned to apologise in Afrikaans for not speaking the language. "Assenblief. Ek kaanet Afrikaans prat" would usually elicit a response in perfect English. Afrikaans' hospitality towards the circus folk was surprising and terrific, once they forgave us for being English.

The three week stand in Jo'burg was strange. It was Christmas and yet it was very hot at 6000 feet above sea level. We moved off the train and into a very basic hotel not far from the tent in Braamfontein. At that time (1957) Braamfontein was a very poor, white working-class area with most of the menial jobs on South African Railways.

Thanks to the Dutch Reform Church we did not work on Sundays or on Christmas Day, but the management made up for that with three shows most other days. The early matinees were hard as the temperature in the tent could reach the nineties (mid-thirties in Degrees Celsius), and we had to get used to working at the high altitude. Both acts were very well received and I was getting used to playing in the band. I had a bit of a crush on Gloria Bale, daughter of Trevor Bale the ringmaster, who had a very high opinion of herself and seemed to exude sex. She did a five-minute spot on the high trapeze while the ring-boys put up the lion cage below.

Our MD thought it would be good for me to play a saxophone solo of the 'Fountains of Rome' for Gloria to perform to. She was in the spotlight and at the end of my solo the other spotlight fell on me to a trickle of applause. I enjoyed it too, but Gloria still ignored me! I think she fancied Roger, the brilliant flyer from the Marylees flying act. He was daring, Mexican and fearless. He was also older and more mature.

During our time in Joburg I was keen to find a piano to play, so one morning on a day when we had no afternoon show, I took the bus into Joburg city centre. I found a music shop and they kindly let me have an hour or so in one of their studio rooms. This became a regular event on matinee-free days. They still had trams in Joburg in 1957, so I tried planning my journeys so that I could ride them whenever possible.

On Christmas Day we exchanged presents over breakfast in the hotel, went to the botanic gardens in the morning and retuned for a fairly basic Christmas lunch at the hotel. On Boxing Day we had three shows, all packed out and enthusiastically received. Toward the end of the three weeks we had got used to the heat and the altitude and settled into a routine, but now it was time to re-join the train for our push towards the coast and Portuguese East Africa (later Mozambique).

Chapter 8

The railway's route between South Africa and Lourenco Marques (now Maputo)), the capital city of Portuguese East Africa, was well used by white South Africans who travelled there to holiday. They enjoyed the freedom and relaxed atmosphere; bars open seven days a week, entertainment on Sundays and Holy days and a less severe form of apartheid.

When the train crossed into Portuguese East Africa, even the countryside looked different. Cousin Colin and I were very taken with the beautiful mixed-race young women. They were really stunning!

Our three carriages of the circus train were placed on a side platform in the main railway station right in the middle of LM. It was great! The city was made up of wide boulevards with many cafes and restaurants that seemed to be open all day and all night.

Boswells worked us very hard here, with three shows a day including Sundays, but we were very relaxed in this easy-going city. Quite often, after the last of the three shows, we would venture out to eat and sit in the bars and cafes until two or three in the morning. Very different from the rigid formality we had to observe in South Africa.

(I was to return to LM, now Maputo, in 2003 with my wife Deborah and daughter Eleanor, who was doing her PhD fieldwork in Malawi, for a vacation. We stayed at the Polana Hotel, a great place to relax and experience the joys of a bygone era).

We were two weeks in Lourenco Marques then we made it back across the frontier into South Africa and north to Bechuanaland and on to Southern Rhodesia where we were to stand in Salisbury (Harare) for two weeks. On the way to these major cities we made one-night stands; very hard work but very interesting too.

The train was crossing the Kruger National Park and in the evening our circus lions would roar and were answered by the wild lions in the park. One travelling afternoon the train had to stop and wait for a large herd of African elephants to cross the track as it would have been dangerous to split the herd.

On another occasion the train was being hauled up a steep incline by two locomotives when one of the wagons housing two elephants broke in two. Neither of the large creatures was injured but a long delay occurred while the front half of the train was moved on to the next junction, the single track cleared of the damaged wagon (with help from the circus elephants who lifted damaged parts from the track). Another locomotive was then sent to pull our back part of the train to join up with the front half. This whole episode took a day and so disrupted the train services between South Africa and Rhodesia that we missed our next one-night stand by two days. It was the only time during the 75,000 miles travelled in the year that we were late for a show!

We duly arrived in the Southern Rhodesian capital of Salisbury (Harare) where we were to play for a week. It was quite a relief to see the Union Jack flying above most large buildings plus a real feeling of patriotism wherever we went and to be free from Afrikaans' hostile attitudes. There was segregation between whites and blacks in Rhodesia but it was not as obvious as in South Africa. There was one similarity with South Africa though: all bars and pubs were closed on Sundays. We were, however, told of a tea shop where the beverages were somewhat stronger than tea and coffee. We found the place easily and having secured a table, placed our order for 'special' tea. When it came, along with four cups and saucers, we noticed that the tea pot was cold: it was full of red wine!

The circus stood on the old cricket ground in Salisbury, which was very well kept and level. The only downside was a plague of grass fleas by which we were severely bitten. The week passed quickly and uneventfully and, on the Sunday, we moved off towards Bulawayo, from Shona country into Ndebele country and stood at Vic Falls for three days during which time we managed a lot of sightseeing. We also built our 'big tiflute' human pyramid right in front of the falls for a publicity photo'.

We crossed the bridge over the Zambezi from Southern to Northern Rhodesia and up through the Copper Belt, heading towards the Congo frontier, when we came, quite unexpectedly, to own a parrot. My dad saw an African man on a bike with a make-do cage on the back containing an African Grey Parrot. The cyclist had come across the border from the Congo to sell the parrot and my dad bought it, much to my mother's opposition. We named the bird Chingola Mufalera after the two villages on the Congo side of the frontier. He was to require medical certificates in quadruple and a work permit when we finally brought him back to the UK as a working parrot to perform in Dick Whittington at the Alhambra Theatre Bradford!

During the next month we made our way back down over the Victoria Falls railway bridge to Southern Rhodesia, on through Bulawayo, Salisbury and back across the frontier with Portuguese East Africa to the port of Beira. It was quite tropical there and we suffered from mosquito bites. Fortunately, we had installed fine netting in the train windows, so a swift insect spray of the train's compartments before going to bed seemed to keep us clear of the night-time biting.

Beira was a huge, active port in the late 50s and the route of many exports and imports from the land-locked Federation of Rhodesia and Nyasaland (Malawi). One of the things I really missed in Africa was Chinese food, so on a day in Beira when we had no afternoon matinee we took two taxis to a highly recommended establishment on the beach out of town. We had a good meal but the food just kept on coming! We ate so much that we had difficulty performing in the evening show. Acrobats should never eat large meals before performing – now I knew why!

Chapter 9

Easter 1958 was fast approaching and we were heading back to South Africa and Durban the capital of Natal Province; it was also the beginning of the rainy season.

After just over five months on tour, spring 1958 marked the return leg of the tour. Though it was the rainy season as we travelled back to South Africa, there were still some entertaining moments. One episode stands out in particular: The tent was pitched on an area of sandy wasteland and the rain fell solidly for the whole two weeks, turning the site into a quagmire. It was very hot and humid too and my cousin Colin was thirsty. He asked one of the ring boys to fetch him a Coke; the young man ran off in the pouring rain and Colin waited and waited. Two hours had passed when the ring boy ran to our dressing room followed closely by a man in a complete chef's outfit; "Here is your cook boss" he shouted! Colin never really lived this one down; his Middlesbrough accent had confused the listener, Cook with Coke.

An encounter with a particularly hot curry also sticks in the memory from this time. Durban had a very large Indian community and some excellent restaurants. My mum and I had a hankering after some spicy food and we were recommended to an excellent Indian restaurant. I was good with chillies and ordered an extra hot Madras curry. The manager suggested very politely that it would be too hot for the young sahib, but I persisted. The staff stood around in amazement while I demolished a whole portion; it was extremely hot. During that night and the following day I regretted being so macho!

On down the east coast to East London and Port Elizabeth, down the Garden Route. Not far from East London we stood at Ooudeshorn for two days. There was an ostrich farm run by a man called Cowboy Jones? We visited at his invitation and had a lot of fun riding the big birds.

As we approached the end of the season the Boswell's management was keen to extend the troupe's tour by another year. This was not to be, however, as we had a firm contract for a 12-week pantomime run in Dick Whittington at the Alhambra Theatre Bradford starring Ronnie Hilton.

Our final show was in Port Elizabeth at the end of November 1958. After fond farewells to our fellow artistes, we boarded a scheduled train for Cape Town to join the SS Sterling Castle for our trip home to Southampton. It was an odd feeling to be going home, with some relief as well as sadness too at leaving southern Africa.

The sea voyage back to the UK was fairly uneventful and as we travelled further north the weather became grey and damp. A year after our departure, we arrived back to another misty November day.

Back to Bradford

What a shock! Two weeks from Cape Town to Southampton. From sunshine to winter fogs. Docking in Southampton, the first man on board was the inspector from the Ministry of Agriculture and Fisheries, to check Chingola the African Grey parrot and stamp his health certificates. "A performing bird, eh? I told him we were bound for pantomime in Bradford; Chingola was to be the captain's parrot in Dick Whittington."

The morning was grey and foggy, the train journey to Waterloo rather depressing. The expectation of a year's looking forward to getting home seemed diminished by the greyness, by the lack of bright sunshine we had become used to in South Africa.

Back to the flat in Fulham, where my aunt Peggy, not a fan of hard housework, had scrubbed the flat clean after the less than desirable tenants had left. It was nice to be back, and we had a few days to settle in before rehearsals in London for the Bradford panto.

Old school friends to catch up with. I took the 22 bus to Putney Common and made for Peter Roberts house. The Roberts had moved from a mansion flat to a house in Clarendon Drive during my year's absence. They were my second family and it was truly great to be reunited once again. Peter was full of plans for Christmas, parties to go to, girls to meet. At the same time, I was beginning to think about my future. Did I want to remain as a performer? My roots were not really in show business and I worked when my friends socialised. I loved my parents dearly, but it was a very restrictive set-up for a 17-year-old boy.

The Roberts were delighted to see me. Peter had left school after disappointing GCE results and was now a young apprentice shop assistant at Simpsons in Piccadilly. He had always been a reasonably smart dresser, but now he wore stiff collars, brilliant white shirts and truly fashionable dark suits. It made him look and behave in a much more mature way. I met him for lunch during his midday breaks, and envied his West End lifestyle.

Back to the flat. Cousin Colin, noticing my lack of enthusiasm for Bradford, encouraged me to think of all those beautiful chorus girls just waiting to be taken by these bronzed, muscular young men from South Africa. He was obsessed with sex. I just wanted to fall in love and thought him immoral in his endless quest for satisfaction. I also secretly admired him and envied his guiltless lifestyle. He matured very early and was a man long before his peer group gave up playing with model trains. I guess I owe him an enormous debt in teaching me the facts of life from a personal point of view. He was more like an elder brother to me than a cousin.

Rehearsals started in premises just off Marylebone Lane, and once we had started, I became more enthusiastic. The star of the show was singer Ronnie Hilton. He was riding high in the charts at the time with 'The Days that the Rain Came Down'. Ronnie was from Leeds, so the Leeds-Bradford audiences would certainly fill the Alhambra Theatre every night. As in previous panto seasons with Dick Whittington, we were to play minor parts in the story along with our acrobatic speciality act 'the Volants'. The opening scene was the Harlequinade. I was the butcher's boy walking across the stage with sausages in a basket. When the thief steals the sausages, he doesn't realise that they are attached by elastic; they come flying back to a great howl from the audience! Cousin Colin was to play the cat, and spent most of the show time in a very warm cat suit.

Off to Bradford on the train. My father had not yet replaced the car he sold before we went to South Africa, the seven of us, plus props and luggage made our way to Kings Cross for the rail journey to Bradford Forster Square. It was foggy when we arrived, late afternoon, in Bradford. Taxis to the Alhambra Theatre, then on to our digs in Manningham Road. The landlady showed us to our respective rooms and we settled in to our home for the next sixteen weeks. Tired after a long day travelling, we retired to bed as we had rehearsals in the theatre at 9am the next day.

It was strange not having my grandmother with us. We had lived as a very close family in very restricted conditions on the circus train in South Africa. Now we had space of our own, and I felt lonely without her. She had made it clear that she wanted to retain her independence at the flat in Buer Road Fulham, and that she would be going to my Aunt Peggy's in Watford for Christmas.

There was great excitement upon arriving at the Alhambra Theatre at 8:30 am for 9 o'clock start. Some of the scenery had already been installed. It was good to be back in a proper variety theatre again. The 22 chorus girls were onstage in their rehearsal gear, some showing a lot more than others. Colin and I were very interested in a blond and a brunette, and did not take long in introducing ourselves. Jenny, and Pauline. We quickly arranged to meet for coffee at the snack bar opposite the stage door, once we knew when a break was coming. With my parents pre-occupied with the production routines and our costumes, I took the opportunity to be off the leash for a while – it was a relief not to be the main object of their attention.

The named members of the cast showed up at about 10am, greeting each other like long lost friends. They were Ronnie Hilton who was top of the bill as Dick Whittington, Sonny Jenks as Dame, Don and Norman as Captain and Mate, Irish comedian Billy Stott as Idle Jack, and Henry Livings as King Rat. Henry, an experienced actor, went on to be a successful playwright and producer.

Chapter 10

After a year in Africa, we were very tanned and, I suppose, handsome. There were 20 dancers in the show and two of them – Maureen and Jenny – made a beeline for Colin and me. During our breaks in dress rehearsals, we all went to the local Milk Bar for refreshments. I was in love (ugh). I guess the girls and Colin were in it for sex, whereas I was just in love; no sex before marriage! This was not what Jenny wanted and our non-relationship instantly became non-existent!

I was heartbroken and my parents were distraught, not knowing how to tell me that Jenny had quickly moved on to the married star of the show Ronnie Hilton. Don Arrol and Ronnie now with Jenny and Maureen were spending non-working time in the hotel opposite the stage door.

I was gated; not allowed out after the evening performances unless with my parents – how demeaning!

In the mornings I used to sneak into the orchestra pit and play the piano. Ronnie Hilton's accompanist Will Fyffe Junior would often listen and complemented me on several occasions; he was a nice man.

The pantomime was fun to be in. We not only did our Volants speciality act but performed throughout the production. Colin played Dick Whittington's cat and Henry Livings was King Rat. The problem with long runs (16 weeks) was boredom and, to alleviate this, we got up to some pranks, which were, of course, strictly forbidden! Just before the finale there was a scene set in Morocco where the Sultan presented Dick and his cat with a box of jewels as a reward for killing all the rats plaguing the country. One afternoon performance we got a stage 'skip' and filled it with stage weights; it took six of us to move it. When the Sultan presented Dick with the jewels, six of us dragged the gold painted skip on to the stage; leaving Ronnie Hilton to exit with it at the end of the scene – he couldn't shift it. This caused major hilarity in the wings and orchestra pit. In the end we helped Ronnie off with the skip and were severely reprimanded by the Stage Manager.

On another occasion, the Dame – Sonny Jenks – swapped places and costumes with the good fairy, all very confusing for the audience but hilarious for the cast!

Our digs about a mile up the hill from the theatre. The landlady was very welcoming but her husband was unusual; he was an undertaker and had a strangely translucent pallor about him! He was always bringing little trinkets home for us. But when we realised where they came from, we stopped accepting these little gifts! On Christmas Day he dressed up in his best morning suit. He carved the turkey and we had all sat down to eat when he picked up the gravy boat and the bottom fell out of it, covering his lap in hot, greasy gravy.

During our stay in Bradford my dad bought a fish and chip shop! I think he wanted very much to carry on where his mother left off; she had a very successful fish and chip restaurant at Cargo Fleet in Middleborough on the approach to the Transporter Bridge. I think this represented one of the few secure times in his life as a small boy, and he wanted to recreate this for us. Sadly, it did not work. He employed our landlady to run it and it never got off the ground. The hard-earned savings from South Africa went overnight!

Our long panto season in Bradford ended in April. We went back to London for a month before heading to Great Yarmouth and the Hippodrome Circus for a 16-week run. We went two weeks early so that new routines for the Volants and the Congas could be rehearsed.

Mum and Dad were keen for me to use my musical skills, so I was to rehearse a solo soprano sax spot. I hated the idea and was filled with dread. Monty Sunshine currently had a top ten hit record with Petit Fleur, so I got the record and learned it note for note from the disc. It actually didn't sound too bad.

43

The musical spot was to open the Congas comedy act: me, in the centre of the ring within the spotlight. Once the main bit of my effort was over, I was to break into the chorus, joined by Colin on banjo, Dave on Bass Drum and my mum on Alto Sax. We were to march round the ring before the chase began: Colin changed into a gorilla costume chasing my mum out of the ring.

On the first dress rehearsal it went well all apart from my solo, which I played well but the audience ignored! Discussions took place with the management and Roberto Germains the ringmaster and they decided that the music solo spot was to be dropped as it was not suitable for this particular show. I was very relieved but felt I should show some disappointment for my parent's sake.

I was now just back in the Volants and my star trick tinskas round, in the dark with UV lighting on. It looked very good and always drew a good round of applause when the lights came up. It was not particularly difficult or dangerous: those other tricks were left to real acrobats!

It was while we were based in Great Yarmouth that I learned to drive. My Dad was a very good instructor and I applied for a driving test in Lowestoft, the nearest test centre. During the Yarmouth season we had driven many miles on Sundays to shows a various Butlins Holiday Camps; from Gt Yarmouth to Pthwelli in North Wales, Filey in Yorkshire. My driving test was to be first thing on a Monday morning, so Dad let me off from a north Wales Butlins show; I stayed in Gt Yarmouth and took a bus to Lowestoft where I walked the town to get to know the street layout for the next morning's driving test. It was a useful thing to do and Dad, who had arrived back with the troupe from Wales at three in the morning, drove me to Lowestoft. We had had a little trouble with the Morris Oxford's handbrake setting and the column gear change lever. We were early for the test, so Dad tightened the handbrake cable.

The driving examiner duly arrived at the test centre and we set off around the town. I thought I had failed on the three-point turn, as the car kept slipping out of reverse. Then, turning left into a very narrow road, I clipped the curb with the rear wheel. He then directed me along a main road at the back of the town, the road bared to the left; straight ahead were large cemetery gates. "Bear left Mr Hutchinson, we don't want to go in there do we?" he commented. Should I laugh or just remain quiet? I opted for the latter. I duly carried out the emergency stop and answered the Highway Code questions. "I'm pleased to tell you that you have passed" he said. I thanked him profusely. "Don't thank me, thank yourself" he snapped at me, handing over the green pass certificate. He got out of the car, slammed the door and seemingly stormed off! I was to learn later that there had been some sort of Payola scandal surrounding the driving test locally; no wonder he was so tetchy.

Chapter 11

As the season in Great Yarmouth drew to a close, I persuaded my parents that they should let me return to my music training at the Central School of Dance Music in London. The troupe would be working odd weeks in the provinces between the end of summer season and pantomime, this year in Sheffield at the Lyceum Theatre; Dick Whittington again but with Tony Dalli as Dick. They reluctantly agreed, so I would be based at the Fulham flat and be able to resurrect my social life.

During this period, in-between my two or three music lessons each week, I earned some money as a film extra; checking in on the phone every day with e FAA (Film Artistes Association). I spent a glorious week on the set of 'Our Man in Havanna' with Alec Guinness and Burl Ives. The set was a recreation of a hotel bar and I was a page boy. It paid really well as it was a cameo part and I was the only extra on the set. Alec Guinness was a real gent, spending a few moments each day before shooting began greeting everyone personally on the set. Sadly it's no use looking for me in the movie as all the bits I was in ended up on the cutting-room floor!

As my London social life began to resume, I was looking forward to spending Christmas with friends and my Grandmother in Fulham. Alas, this was not to be! I got a phone call from Dad to say that Carole, one of the troupe had broken her arm and would be out of action for some weeks. "Would I take her place in the Volants at Sheffield for at least the first part of the Panto season," he asked? Of course I agreed and we immediately went into pre-rehearsal in London before travelling to Sheffield at the end of November.

Chapter 12

Sheffield at Christmas in 1959 was really quite enjoyable; it had one of the only remaining old-style tramway systems too, which I rode many times during our stay.

The Christmas season was not as pressured for me as I was only a stand-in for Carol, so there were no unwanted expectations from my parents. The Lyceum Theatre was a nice place and I soon settled into the old routines. Toni Dalli, a former Sheffield steel worker with a beautiful voice was top of the bill. His big hit single had shot him to stardom. He tended to keep his private life to himself, so we did not get to know him as well as we had got to know Ronnie Hilton in Bradford the previous year. I always felt it was a shame, as in later years Toni opened a restaurant in Marbella not far from our Spanish apartment near Gibraltar.

The Sheffield digs we stayed in were okay but the landlady was rather mean. It was a cold winter and she seriously rationed the coal for our sitting room fire. In the end we took to burning whatever we could, just to keep warm. The food she provided was very basic: lots of mashed potatoes and very little meat. We always ate our main meal of the day after the last show, so at about 11pm. That is also when we wanted a warm room to sit in and relax, hence the search for anything to burn when the small amount of coal ran out!

As usual, the panto season was 12 weeks and by week six Carol was back and rehearsing to take my place in the act. We changed places midweek and I was soon on the train bound for St Pancras, Fulham, music lessons and my regained social life. It was good to be back living in the flat with my grandmother but my lust for a normal life was not to be granted for long.

To earn some money I checked in with the FAA each day to see if there was any film extra work. The answer was generally a bit but not much. One Monday morning, just as I was about to leave the flat for the Central School of Dance Music, the phone rang. It was the Deputy Stage Manager from the London Coliseum, where my Dad had four acrobats in Harold Fielding's production of Aladdin. There was a problem and since my dad was away in Sheffield, it was me they turned to for help. They asked me to come in to the theatre as soon as possible: one of the acrobats had broken his arm and couldn't work.

By 2:30 pm that same Monday I was on stage, in a production I had never seen, with people I didn't know. The show starred Doretta Morrow, Ian Wallace and Bob Monkhouse. The reason for my panic enrolment in the production was that Doretta's first entrance as princess was on a podium carried by four strong acrobats. It would not work with only three, and the male dancers in the show 'couldn't possibly shoulder such a burden dahling'!

Everyone was very friendly and welcoming and grateful to me for filling in at such short notice, especially Doretta Morrow. Mum and Dad were really pleased too, as they relied on the additional income from the show. The acrobats, Fred Leopold Snr, Freddie Leopold Jnr, and Max Regelski were also relieved that I had arrived; Ted Jones was the one injured. Initially, I just carried the podium in the opening sequence, but gradually got incorporated into the rest of the production, performing my tinskas round over the spears of the royal guards: quite difficult. The only bit I could not do was a front cloth routine with Ian Wallace, where on command he clapped his hands and the acrobats stood on their hands until, after a minute or so, he clapped again and they stood back on their feet again. I could not stand on my hands with any certainty for any period of time. Practice as I may I couldn't master it, so they left me out of that scene. It was nice to be working in the West End, and I got on well with the two Freds and Max. They had all worked for Dad at some time or another.

I was just leaving the flat one morning about a week after starting at the Coliseum when the postman delivered a rather important looking letter addressed to me. It was from Harold Fielding, personally topped and tailed by him, thanking me for stepping into the show at such short notice and saving the day. He said that if there was ever anything he could do to help me in my career, I shouldn't hesitate to contact him. An offer that both he and I might live to regret!

Towards the end of the season Ted Jones was well enough to re-join Aladdin, so I rather sadly gave way to him and prepared to resume my musical training, although I had a nagging thought that I would never hit the standard of playing I'd be satisfied with. Should I think of another career path, maybe in management? I rather fancied a shot at the production side, so maybe I would take up Harold Fielding's offer? I found my Dad's old portable typewriter and composed a thoughtful letter to Harold. I took a 14 bus to Green Park and walked through Berkeley Square to 13 Bruton Street, the offices of Harold Fielding Ltd where I personally hand delivered the letter to reception. Two days later I answered the phone "Renown 4831, can I help you?" It was Harold Fielding's secretary to say I should come to see him and Ray Gammon, who was Production Manager.

I was thrilled and quite nervous; I wore my best Sidney Fisher suit and turned up 15 minutes early for the interview. A kind man, Harold Fielding immediately put me at ease. He introduced me to Ian Bevan who ran the artistes' agency and looked after Tommy Steele who was a big star at the time. I was then taken to meet Ray Gammon who was quite amused that I should want to work at the other side of the footlights. "We can offer you a job as Ray's assistant" Harold said. "You'll be on his coat tails from 9 am to 11 pm most days, just depending on how many shows we have running at the time. Hopefully you'll learn quickly and be able to stand in as an ASM (assistant stage manager) to cover sickness and holiday absences. We'll pay you fifteen guineas a week. We do, however, have a problem: we have five Brians in the organisation, the chief one being our star company manager

49

Brian Pender, so we'll have to call you something else – how about Johnny – after your Dad?" That was quite a shock; I get a new job and then lose my own identity and adopt my Dad's name! I desperately wanted the job, so I agreed, but it took quite a while before I would immediately respond to 'Johnny'!

Harold Fielding Productions had a series of high profile shows on in London. *The Music Man* starring Van Johnson at the Adelphi, *Most Happy Fella* at the Coliseum, *Progress Through the Park* at the Saville directed by the very difficult Tim O'Brien, and *Houseboat* in Kashmir at the Savoy. I attended all the pre-production meetings with Ray Gammon and Jimmy Bailey the chief carpenter. I met and got to know Michael Northern the lighting director, J Hutchinson-Scott the set designer a really nice man with a splendid house just off the King's Road in Chelsea.

The Music Man required liquid carbon dioxide for the steam effects, so two mornings a week I drove the company's black Bedford van out to Park Royal with an empty gas cylinder and collected a full one, returning to the Adelphi stage door in Maiden Lane with my delivery. The workers at the gas plant thought I was far too posh (me posh?) to be driving a van, but they were very nice really and supplied me with tea and a bacon roll at each visit free of charge. One evening, between the end of the matinee and the evening show, I was standing in the prompt corner chatting to Peter Toft, the Adelphi's stage carpenter. Peter was an angry man and often said things out loud that the rest of us just kept to ourselves. Suddenly Van Johnston appeared next to us. "Do you guys know that the tannoy is switched on and everyone can hear what you are discussing?" It was nice of him to warn us, and I would certainly be more discrete in future!

I spent most evenings on the side of the stage at one of the theatres, learning the ropes. Brian Pender was a real whizz, following the script and cueing the lighting, the tabs and the sound effects. I was not sure I could ever cope with that sort of responsibility, but he loved it. I also worked alongside Joan Preston, equally skilled but quite a different style to Brian.

Some Saturday nights were taken up with 'get outs' and 'get ins' of productions from big London theatres. The get out from the Saville of a production was really quite enjoyable. Being in the West End at 3 am on a Sunday was strange as there were very few people about. Not like today when it seems that the 24/7 culture has taken over. When all was packed away in the trucks, Jimmy Bailey would lead the search for an early morning café and a big fry-up for all. There was a lot of camaraderie amongst the production team on occasions like these.

It was during my time with HFP that I first met my wife Deborah, on one of the few weekends off. Through my old friend Peter Roberts, I had met Hugh Macintosh, nephew of Barbara Castle and son of Marjorie Macintosh who chaired the education committee at the GLC. They were an interesting, intellectual Labour family. On this particular Saturday afternoon in the height of a glorious summer, Hugh and I were standing outside his family's house just off Putney Common, when this girl with the longest legs I'd ever seen cycled up. She was wearing the shortest gymslip I had ever seen and was returning from playing hockey for Putney High School. "This is Deborah Main, a very dear friend of mine" said Hugh. "We've been invited to a party at someone's house in Wimbledon tonight, so Deborah, will you come too?" I had the use of my dad's Morris Oxford estate car so offered to give everyone a lift there and back.

I picked Peter and Hugh up from Clarendon Drive and Hugh directed me to Gwendolen Avenue, a wide residential street with large detached Victorian houses. Number 30 was on the corner of Gwendolen and St John's Avenue. I had the window down; Hugh got out and rang the bell. Deborah, smiling, got in the back seat with Hugh, "Whose van is this?" she asked. I replied that it was my father's estate car. Van indeed! I reckoned she needed pulling down a peg or two!

We then picked up Dave Waite and Janet Greenfield and made our way to Wimbledon and the party. We got a lot of party invites mainly due to our musical efforts. Dave Waite and Roger Evans both played guitar and were really good folk singers, Janet too had a lovely voice. They often guested on the Tonight programme on BBC 1 which was hosted by Cliff Michelmore. I had brought my clarinet in the car and we were soon at the party providing the music. One of our favourite pieces was the theme from *Black Orpheus* which sounds great when the melody is played on clarinet.

It was during this musical interlude that I noticed Deborah looking at me and smiling. I thought then that she was as attracted to me as I was to her. I had not made any approach as I thought she was Hugh's girlfriend and chaps did not do that! The party ended at about 1 am and I dropped Hugh home, then Deborah. We exchanged phone numbers and said we would get in touch soon.

The following Monday morning I arrived at Bruton Street at 9 am and spent the time before lunch at pre-production meetings for *Progress Through the Park* which was opening that week at the Saville Theatre in Shaftesbury Avenue. Final dress rehearsal was on the Wednesday evening and my boss, Ray Gammon, asked whether I could rustle up some numbers for the audience? What a great excuse to contact Deborah; I dialled PUTney 1696 and waited. "This is Ursula Main, can I help you?" I asked to speak to Deborah but was told she was out; so I left a message saying that I had up to four tickets for the show and would she call me if she wanted to come.

I had arranged to meet Peter Roberts for lunch that day, so I duly turned up at the staff entrance to Simpsons in Jermyn Street. Peter was on early lunch, so at 12 noon he appeared and we set off for Rupert Street where one of the Chinese restaurants offered a cheap lunch 2/6d for three courses!

Back at the office and a message from Deborah, she and her sister Ursula would like tickets. I rang the Saville box office and asked them to put two front circle seats in an envelope to be collected by Deborah Main. I called Deborah's number and left a message on the answering machine/answerphone.

I was really enjoying my time with HFP and the possibility of a developing relationship with Deborah. She said that she enjoyed the play at the Saville and we agreed to meet up again soon. I felt excited and very apprehensive.

Life at home with my grandmother and my parents (when they were in London) had settled down to a calm routine and the pressure from my mum and dad to re-join them in the acts had vanished, for the time being anyway. I guess that to have their only child working for the number one impresario in London theatre was the next best thing to performing: at least I was in the business!

I had been at HFP for nearly a year when Ray Gammon dropped a bombshell one morning: he had suggested to Harold that I should stage manage the touring companies when they went national at the end of the London seasons! My relationship with Deborah was growing into what I thought could be a long-lasting one however, and the last thing I wanted was to be away for months on end. Indeed, prolonged travelling was one of the reasons that I had stopped working for my dad.

Poor Ray thought he was doing me a favour and was quite knocked back when I wasn't keen. The problem was that he had presented it to Harold as a certainty and there was no going back. I would seriously have to re-assess my position.

Deborah then dropped bombshell number two: she was going to Norway for six weeks in the summer as companion to the wife of a seriously wealthy ship owner. I couldn't help thinking that it was her parents' behind it; wanting to get her away from me before the relationship became too serious. Summer was fast approaching, so what was I to do? I spent a tearful day in the flat, wondering if it would last.

The next day we were on the coach to Blackpool, it took 9 hours on the stopping service! My poor mother had been waiting at Blackpool coach station for ages as she thought we were on the direct service from London which had arrived many hours earlier. Having got over that, we took a taxi to the flat my parents had rented for the season and unpacked our bags. Then down to the North Pier Theatre where the act was appearing. The show had just finished and we went off to 'the' fish and chip restaurant for supper. It was good to see Mum and Dad and cousin Colin too, and for a short while I was able to forget my sadness at being separated from Deborah.

We settled in to life in Blackpool and my parents were very sensitive to my predicament. I spent some evenings at the Pier Theatre, some seeing other Blackpool shows, while other evenings were spent at the flat, watching TV with my grandmother and playing with Chingola the parrot. Blackpool still has trams today, running along the seafront, but in those days the trams also ran through the town and several routes passed by the flat. My grandmother and I spent some time riding these trams, reminding ourselves of past years in London when on Friday nights we would do our boat, tram and bus outings.

I wrote to Deborah every day – long thoughtful letters. I waited and waited for a reply. Ten days later it came. I still have all her letters today but am somewhat embarrassed to read mine to her.

My Dad bought some fishing tackle and on Sundays, when there were no shows, we would drive into the beautiful Lancashire countryside to fish, taking a picnic with us. It was nice but many years later my parents still spoke of my misery and how they gave up trying to cheer me up in the end.

And then the question finally came up that my parents had surely been itching to ask since my arrival: would I re-join the act? They knew I was missing Deborah and they probably thought it was just a repeat of my foolish behaviour with the dancers Jenny Mee, Jean Atkinson and Yvonne de Vinter. This time I knew it was for real.

I explained that I really did not want to be a performer and that, when the time came, I would like to return to London with my grandmother and find a job. I think this was devastating for both of them. It was hard for them to accept that their only son would not become a star.

On returning to London I got on the phone straight away and found out that Deborah was back in Putney. We met at Gwendolen Avenue; her parents were away and her siblings were out. It was a nervous meeting for both of us. Deborah was not sure whether I felt the same as I did before the summer. I had written to her every day during our separation, so thought she should have no doubt!

We finally embraced and made plans for the rest of the summer holiday before she returned to Putney High School's Upper Sixth Form for her 'A' levels.

Chapter 13

During the times when Deborah and I were not together I tried to find a job. Vernon Phillips, my uncle, was a senior manager with North Thames Gas, so I thought I would ask him if there were any job interviews with the company. He was not terribly helpful but told me that there was an advertisement for trainees in the *Fulham Chronicle*. I applied and was invited to take a test and an interview.

I passed the written test and was interviewed by a rather austere man who said that as I had been an acrobat and now wanted to work for the gas board, that I would have to undergo a medical examination. I guess the implication was that I'd given up being an acrobat due to ill health. He gave me a date and time. That was it for me: I telephoned his secretary and withdrew my application. I later learned that Vernon was surprised and disappointed that I had not accepted a job!

My Aunt Peggy got in touch later that week to tell me that there was an advert in the *Evening Standard* for an administration assistant at the Royal College of Music. Was I interested? she wondered. I got the paper and phoned the bursar, Captain Shrimpton. The vacancy was still open. Shrimpton asked me to attend an interview the next day. My grandmother was very pleased and offered to accompany me to Kensington. She would have a coffee while I was interviewed.

We got the District Line from Putney Bridge to Kensington High Street where she found a café and I set off for the RCM which was immediately behind the Royal Albert Hall in Prince Consort Road.

Captain Shrimpton offered me the job after about five minutes of conversation. I think I was the only person to apply! He took me to meet my prospective boss, Percy Showan, who ran the General Office where all the timetables for students and professors were created. Percy was a great character and doubled between the RCM and Sadler's Wells, where he was Assistant Orchestral Manager. I soon learned that he and his wife lived just off Munster Road in Fulham and that Mrs Showan was UK women's' croquet champion. There were three desks in the General Office; Percy's, Michael McCabe's and mine. Michael was a very quiet and thoughtful person who could complete the *Telegraph*'s most difficult crosswords in about ten minutes; what was he doing as an admin manager at the RCM?

I soon got into the swing of things at the RCM. Percy was rather easy going as long as you delivered and Mac was very kind and patient as I learned the ropes. They liked my copperplate writing and I was soon writing up the professors' timetable books which were updated at the beginning of each term. (They are still in the basement vault of the RCM to this day!).

The daily routine was to arrive at 0900 and open the office. We kept all the keys for the tuition rooms and practice rooms, so life was quite busy from the start. I was introduced to various members of the teaching staff and I gradually got to know them by name. When I first arrived, the guitarist John Williams was a student but by the next term he had been appointed a professor. There were many famous people: Sir Malcolm Sergeant used to take the First Orchestra for rehearsals and concerts. He was not the easiest person to deal with and lived in Albert Hall Mansions just across the road. One afternoon, following a rehearsal for the First Orchestra, I clearly remember him strutting into the entrance hall, giving the hall porter, who limped with a bad leg, his small briefcase and ordering the poor man to follow him across the road and up the twenty steps to Albert Hall Mansions.

Another real character was Oswald Peasgood, sub-organist at Westminster Abbey. The story goes that he was a far better organist than the principal organist but that his penchant for motor bikes and dirty jokes was a barrier to his elevation to that position. He could be playing the most difficult Vidor fugues at the same time as telling his guests in the organ loft the dirtiest of jokes. He was very kind to me, offering me his very beat-up Renault Gordini when he got a new car!

Fred Brown was the resident caretaker and engineer at the College, living in a basement flat. We became very friendly; he liked Percy and his General Office staff but did not like the Director's office staff or those in the Finance Office. Fred was very helpful during the long summer holiday period when we admin staff got the same time off as the teaching staff and on full pay.

Chapter 14

In my spare time from the RCM I teamed up with guitarist/folksinger Roger Evans to try writing some theme tunes. He would bring his guitar to Fulham two evenings a week and we would try things out on piano, guitar and clarinet.

This was also an opportunity to make amends to my parents for my failure of ambition to become a star! Dad had been to see Val Parnell, who was the boss of ATV at the time, with an idea for a children's TV series called the *Handy Gang*; him, Dave Jackley and Jack Edwardes; Montmerency of *Mick (Charlie Drake) and Montmerency*. The story goes that VP offered Dad a house or a TV pilot, he went for the pilot. I suggested to Dad that Roger and I could write a theme tune. He agreed and we set to work. Having created the melody, we needed a demo; this is where Fred Brown came in!

The theme's melody needed a harpsichord. It was the summer vacation at the College so Fred offered one of the practice rooms in the College and we brought in a tape recorder. Roger and I worked hard and produced a really catchy tune. By that time, Dad's agent Norman Murray was involved and he negotiated a one-off fee of £100 for the piece. We duly sent him the tape and he sent it on to the musical director for ATV.

I attended their final rehearsal to hear the band play our tune. It sounded really good. The pilot was to be recorded in front of a live audience at the Golder's Green Hippodrome on a Wednesday evening. Roger came to the College at 5 pm and Dad turned up in the Morris Oxford estate car to collect us at 5:30pm. I really felt that this was the beginning of a career writing theme tunes and jingles.

To be frank, the pilot was not very good but Dad seemed pleased and the director said he thought it would be accepted. He, too, liked the theme tune. Sadly, within a week or two, Val Parnell rang Dad to say that ATV did not have a suitable children's' slot for the Handy Gang but that he had suggested to Norman Murray that he should send it to Associated Rediffusion. ATV had the weekend franchise for London whilst AR had weekdays and more scope for children's programmes.

There ensued a long wait of about seven weeks after which Norman phoned Dad with the good news that AR would go with seven episodes to be networked at 5 pm on Wednesdays. The bad news was that AR did not want our theme tune: they had one of their own pre-recorded in their library and published by them, and they wanted the royalties! Because we had signed a one-off deal with ATV, they now owned our copyright and would not release it to AR. This was disappointing but since other parts of my life were going well – at work and with Deborah, I didn't spend long dwelling on this set-back.

Chapter 15

My relationship with Deborah was going well and her family seemed to accept me. Both her parents were psychoanalysts. Her father, Tom Main, was the medical director of the Cassel Hospital for Nervous Disorders on Ham Common. Her mother, Molly Main, was a child psychiatrist working for Richmond Council Social Services. Tom was a controversial figure in the NHS: he spoke his mind and didn't really care whether he upset people or not. Molly was a quietly strong and gentle person, somewhat bullied by her husband. Together they made a striking couple.

Deborah's siblings were Jennifer (Jem), Ursula (Modge) and Andrew. When I first met them, Jem was a medical student at Charing Cross, Deborah and Modge were at Putney High School, and Andrew was at St Paul's.

A weekday evening meal at Gwendolen Avenue could sometimes be likened to a scene from the movie *Gladiator*. Tom Main ruled the roost and the pecking order of the other family members varied according to his mood and the various subjects for discussion. He would frequently make a controversial statement that he did not believe in or agree with just to get a discussion, or more usually an argument, going. At work he was Medical Director of the Cassel and a pioneer psycho-analyst in the area of family therapy. But it was this same outspokenness that I understand cost him a knighthood, despite an outstanding career. At home however, he usually ignored Molly, agreed with and promoted Jem's ideas, confronted Modge and baited her, gave Andrew an easy ride, and trod very carefully with Deborah. I was quite shocked at first, never having had a meal in such a battlefield. I gradually got used to it and was a regular, welcome attendee at Molly's table. She was an excellent cook.

It was a very snowy Christmas in 1963. My Dad was working at the London Palladium in *Little Old King Cole* with Charlie Drake. I wanted to spend time with my folks *and* with Deborah, so I had to tread carefully over the Yuletide period, not to upset my parents. I was pretty good at this as the well-trodden snowy path between the flat at Buer Road Fulham and Gwendolen Avenue Putney would show.

What next career-wise? I really enjoyed my time at the RCM, but there was very little opportunity to progress and the pay was very low. I thought I would like to try my hand in music publishing, but how would I break into this field? Through a contact of my father's, it turned out. My Dad's circus agent, Roberto Germains, worked out of the Noel Gay Organisation in Denmark Street (Tin Pan Alley). Noel Gay was owned by Richard Armitage, whose father, Noel Gay (Armitage), a former student at the RCM, wrote many popular tunes in the 1930/40s. Amongst them was *Run Rabbit Run*, *When the Lights Go Up in London* and *Lambeth Walk*. Richard was Eton and Cambridge educated and close to the Footlights at the university. Along with Noel Gay Music he operated Noel Gay Artists, Noel Gay Productions, and Noel Gay Promotions; the latter run for him by Raman Subba Row the former cricketer. The Noel Gay Organisation had an executive training scheme so, after a chat with Roberto, I wrote to Richard Armitage.

For a while I heard nothing, so continued at the College and enjoyed their long vacations. Tom and Molly Main were away a lot in the summer, so Deborah and I enjoyed life at Gwendolen Avenue. Then one morning a letter arrived from Raman Subba Row inviting me to an interview.

On the day of the interview I took time off from the RCM. With my latest Fisher suit, dark grey and very smart, new shoes and a haircut I looked very good. At the appointed interview hour I entered the reception area of the Noel Gay Organisation and was soon with Raman Subba Row himself. He was charming and fully aware just how nervous I was. The interview lasted half an hour and went well enough for him to call Richard Armitage on the internal phone and I was soon being escorted down to the first floor to meet Richard.

Wearing thick rimmed glasses and sitting behind a large desk was the man I would work closely with for the next eight years. He was sort of screwed up in his reclining desk chair and kept fiddling with his Adams apple, almost as if he had a tick. He told me that Roberto Germains had highly recommended me and that he, Richard, had met and was aware of my dad's work. I was to be paid £20 a week (£1000 a year!), more than my boss Percy Showan was paid at the RCM after many years of service. I would also have an expense allowance of £5 a week.

He told me he would call me 'Hutch' and that he expected to be called Mr Armitage or 'Sir' except in the company of Americans, when I could call him Richard and he would refer to me as Brian. Americans, he said, got offended by surnames! I told him that I had to give six weeks' notice to the College, so I would start work in Denmark Street in October 1963.

I dashed home, full of excitement, to deliver the good news to my parents. Along with my grandmother, they were genuinely pleased for me, asking all sorts of questions. I was aware that my dad was not that keen on Richard, having met him on several occasions with Roberto: Too posh and not very friendly, was my father's view, but he felt sure I could deal with Richard! In a strange way Richard was to fill the gaps that my dad left out and he would become a deputy father-figure to me over time.

The next day I asked to see Percy alone and handed in my notice. He was as sad as I was: my time at the RCM had given me a taste of university life for two years and allowed me to stabilise my life.

Chapter 16

And so, a new chapter of my professional life began, with a tour promoting Gallaghers cigarettes. Tobacco advertising was about to be banned from television and Raman had come up with the idea of touring promotion shows to advertise cigarettes. *The Park Drive Show* and the *Kensitas Show* starring Mike and Bernie Winters were the flagship projects and the venues were the dozen or so Butlins Holiday Camps throughout the UK. We were to travel by bus and play a different camp each day, which sounds simple but the buses were old and slow and the whole thing was a nightmare.

Touring with these shows meant being away from Deborah: I didn't like that a bit! It was all very emotional for me. The BBC was screening the life of the composer Elgar and the theme tune was his 'Salut d'Amour'. I bought the LP and played it over and over again.

Luckily for me, but not for Raman's business, the sponsored shows were not successful and soon came to an end. I had been with Promotions for three months and now it was time to move on to Noel Gay Productions, run by Richard and producer John Lyndon. Mainly involved in Summer Shows, such as *Llandudno* starring Russ Conway and Bournemouth starring Mike and Bernie Winters.

Richard was keen to find out how much I had learned when I worked for Harold Fielding Productions. He quizzed me at length about costs and gate income and did not seem overly impressed with my responses. Russ was also doing Sunday Concerts and I accompanied Richard and his long-time financial director Ralph Walker down to Bournemouth in the Bentley. On the journey Richard asked me how I would react if Terry (Russ) propositioned me. I said, without hesitation, that I would flatten him! I knew that Terry was gay but I also had my doubts about Richard himself. This subject was never mentioned again and it created a minor rift between Richard and me which was to last for the whole 8 years that I worked for him.

Following on from Summer Shows, Richard had Russ Conway and Mike and Bernie Winters doing the Her Majesties Theatres in Glasgow and Edinburgh. His company Stage Manager Bert Maurice was due for a break, so I was to fill in for him. Off to Glasgow then and into digs with Bernie Winters. Terry (Russ) was topping the bill and Mike and Bernie were to close the first half. The two comics didn't hit it off with Terry and found a way of really annoying him. The Watch Committees in Scotland, who controlled entertainment licenses, insisted that the shows must finish at 10:30 pm sharp. Mike and Bernie, who were really popular in Scotland, deliberately extended their spot at the end of the first half, so that Terry had to truncate his second half performance, swearing, not at M & B, but at me as Company Manager for not controlling my artistes! It bugged me a lot at first but then I just decided to take it in my stride – after all, the shows were grossing £8K a week, most of which went into Terry's pocket. Sharing digs with Bernie Winters meant a whole procession of dancing girls passing through the flat in the night. If I'd not been so attached myself it would have been paradise!

With my three months with Productions was coming to an end I had to look to the future. Next up was Noel Gay Music which had a rather old fashioned between-the-wars image; not unnaturally, as Noel Gays songs: *Run Rabbit Run, When the Lights Come Up in London*, and *Lambeth Walk*, were the financial base and success of the group of companies.

The music company was run by the Falconers, husband and wife team, with Jimmy Gordon as Promotion Manager. It was his job to get the records in which NGM had a publishing interest played on the radio and the sheet music translated into arrangements for BBC orchestras to play in such programmes as *Friday Night is Music Night* on the then *Light Programme*.

At this time NGM was having a successful run with Bernard Cribbins *Right Said Fred* and Russ Conway's *Sidesaddle*.

There was, however, some modernising light at the end of the tunnel. Norman Newell, one of the successful group of A & R men at EMI who was involved with Russ Conway's success, had discovered a young duo at Westminster School – Peter Asher and Gordon Waller. Peter's sister Jane Asher was in a relationship with Paul McCartney; he was living part of the time at the Ashers' house in Upper Wimpole Street.

Paul and John Lennon had written a song *World Without Love* and given it to Peter and Gordon to record. Norman Newell and his assistant John Burgess had produced an immediate hit. This was my first big record promotion job and I was glad that I had developed a good working relationship with Roy Featherstone, Head of Marketing and Promotion at EMI Records.

In those days, the mid-1960s, Radio 1 was the main route to singles sales, along with the pirates London and Caroline. It was also possible to get a slot for unknowns on Top of the Pops if there was a strong record and a good connection: Paul and John provided this! I had never been so busy and the Radio 1 producers at Egton House were now pleased to see me. It was a bit different from Cribbins and Conway!

There were the really nice producers: Brian Willey – Saturday Club, Johnny Beerling and others. There were also the really difficult ones and Ron Belchier was the worst. He produced a live lunchtime slot on Radio 1 where Top 20 artistes' singles were performed live with a session band. It was obviously difficult to get the band parts arranged in time, so the BBC would employ a copyist to do this from the record. When it came to Peter and Gordon's' turn it was a disaster; the arranger had written the band parts in E flat and P & G played and sung in E! They got through it in the end but Ron Belchier blamed the duo for the error when in fact it was the BBC arranger's mistake. Ron never engaged Peter & Gordon again even though they had follow-up chart hits!

I travelled to Manchester with Peter and Gordon where Top of the Pops was recorded in a converted church on Thursdays for transmission on Fridays. Johnnie Stewart, the producer, was a really nice person and the boys' slot went well. It was also accepted that some acts doing TOTPs in Manchester would also do 'Scene at 6:30' on the local Granada TV channel. This was produced by Johnny Hamp who had been very involved in the emergence of the Liverpool scene and was close to Brian Epstein who managed not just the Fab Four but Cilla Black and Gerry and the Pacemakers.

In those days Johnny Hamp was a real Manchester party animal and I have many memories of extraordinary parties at a rather dubious hotel called Milverton Lodge. George Best also had a club in the centre of Manchester where we often ended up at the end of a long day.

In the meantime, Deborah and I were married in 1965. Her parents had to accept the fact that she would not be marrying a fellow medic but a former acrobat and musician! They were magnanimous and provided a good wedding. We were married at St Andrews on Ham Common, just a short walk across the Common from the Cassel Hospital, where the reception was held.

In 1969 I moved from Noel Gay to set up Warner Bros Records with Ian Ralfini, Martin Wyatt, Tony Roberts, and Des Brown. In 1970 I found myself once again involved with Peter Asher who was producing and managing James Taylor. In 1970 our first daughter Sophie was born on the day that I had James doing a slot for Peter Carr on BBC 2. I well remember frantically driving back and forth between St Mary's Hospital and the BBC TV Centre until Sophie was born in the evening. Deborah had a fairly rough time but she and Sophie were settled by 10 pm and I headed off to the Main's house in Gwendolen Avenue Putney. I hadn't eaten all day and Molly did me the biggest fry-up I've ever had!

Once Deborah and Sophie were home and settled, many visitors arrived at Burntwoocd Grange Road including Peter and Betsy with a lovely antique silver spoon: it was a joyous time.

Chapter 17

The music business in 1960s – '70s London was a small community of professional production and promotion people. It would take a whole book to mention all the various players but here are a few.

Ronnie Beck was the working end of Feldmans Music Publishers; he looked after many writers and producers one of whom was Mike Leander, a staff producer at Decca Records and a song writer too. Mike wrote the follow-up single to *World Without Love*, Peter and Gordon's No 1 single. This follow-up was not brilliant but got great airplay on the BBC thanks to Ronnie Beck's contacts and mine too! It made the charts but not the Top 5.

I had been involved in other hits when I was at Noel Gay; Paul Jones' Bad Boy (also written by Mike Leander?) which made the Top 10? The Scaffold's Lilly the Pink and Thank You Very Much, also Top Ten hits.

I also had a brief working relationship with Janis Ian. Richard Armitage had set up a management company in New York run by Jean Powell who used to work with me in the London office. The office/ apartment was at 130 W57th in New York, just down from Carnegie Hall and the Russian Tea Rooms. He rented from lawyer Paul Marshall who looked after EMI in the States. Jean was to go on tour with Janis who had just had a huge hit with 'At Seventeen' in the USA. Richard wanted me to look after the office in New York while Jean was on tour. I was very keen to do this as Deborah was doing part of her internship out at Windsor for six weeks during which time we would see very little of each other.

Chapter 18

Though the purpose of my trip to New York was to look after the office while Jean was on tour there, when I arrived in August Jean was out of town. The steam was gushing from pipes in the streets, it was very humid and hot, just like you see in the movies. My first morning there I was really jet-lagged and woke early. I left the hotel and made for a breakfast bar, where I was the first customer of the day. I was struck by the chrome and neon lights. I sat on a tall red bar stool and the barman approached. "Yer, what can I get you?". I hesitated, big mistake, and he was gone. Another customer had come in now. "What can I get you?". There was an immediate response "Bagel, two eggs over-easy, coffee, and make it quick! Right away sir," said the server. I was a quick learner when food was concerned, so when the waiter eventually came back to me, I had rehearsed in my mind and ordered pancakes with maple syrup but I was not brave enough to add the "make it quick". I thought I was going to enjoy New York!

Ian Ralfini had given me an introduction to a former secretary of his, Sue Thompson who now worked for Columbia Records (CBS) in the Black Rock. It was good to have a local person and she introduced me to many people. She was the person who got me to see Linda Ronstadt with the Stone Ponies in a small NY club before she was famous.

I eventually persuaded Jean to let me live in the apartment while she was away with Janis. At first she refused but then saw the sense when Richard Armitage pointed out to her on the 'phone from London that my hotel bills would be charged against her profits. Having the use of an office and apartment in New York was a dream come true. What an exciting place!

At 130 W57th Paul Marshall, Richard's lawyer, had a really nice Japanese lawyer working with him, so he introduced me to small Japanese restaurants where he and his Japanese expat friends ate: cheap and really authentic unlike the many Hibachi houses which were just tourist traps and very expensive.

Jean Powell was now back with Janis Ian in NY for a few days, so I finally got to meet her. Janis was a striking looking teenager. She was also kind of out of control, wrestling on the office carpet with a girlfriend who travelled with her on tour. It was difficult to liken this out of control Tom Boy with the mature and talented singer songwriter she was.

Jean took me to meet Janis's agent at William Morris: a very young and pushy David Geffen. I needed strong representation in New York for Paul Jones as the film *Privilege* was about to premier in the USA. I was to have many dealings in the future with David when he and Elliot Roberts set up Geffen Roberts Management looking after Joni Mitchell, Neil Young, Crosby, Stills and Nash and the Eagles, on which more later.

I was very keen to see Janis in concert, so Jean suggested that I join them a day or so later in Buffalo, a short flight from La Guardia to the shores of Lake Toronto. I flew up on Mohawk Airlines in a small jet plane. The stewardess, an extremely attractive black woman, offered me coffee. "How do you take it?" she asked. I replied that I'd like it black and she rebuked me immediately saying I should say without milk. I had no idea people could be so touchy! Janis's concert was a sell-out. She was great, and grown men in the audience were tearful at her live rendition of *At Seventeen*.

Towards the end of August, I had to plan my return to London. My folks were working in Vegas at the Tropicana Hotel for a year, so I decided to pay them a visit before returning to England. It was great to see Mum and Dad. They really loved working in Vegas and were there for a year with their speciality act *The Herculeans*. We lounged by the pool, did all the shows including theirs and shopped 'til we dropped without seeing a single clock in the town. I remember rehearsing with them round the pool, much like we used to with Boswells Circus in South Africa. I could still do my tinskas round, on the spot, and tinska turns – one or two handed. I still have the 8m cine film from Vegas which also shows my Dad and Brian Lovering having a cross-trick competition. Dad was twice Brian's age but still able to beat him every time!

As my Mum was not in the show, we made a roundtrip via my Aunt Margo and Uncle Bill's home in San Diego. Their daughter, my cousin Linda was also there, as were Stella and John Stafford. Their eldest daughter Ann had been my best friend and neighbour when we all lived in Buer Road Fulham. I had not seen Ann for years and was very shocked at how huge she had become. At that time I was not particularly slim, but she was enormous.

After a couple of days in San Diego my Mum flew back to Vegas and I flew via New York back to London; I had been away for six weeks and was really looking forward to seeing Deborah after so long. She had finished her house job at Windsor and was back at St Mary's Paddington.

Chapter 19

My working life was very much focused on the Pop scene and this is how I had become friendly with Ian Ralfini who ran Robbins Music at that time. His father Jan Ralfini was a successful band-leader. Because my name was linked to Peter and Gordon's' success, Ian asked me to represent a new duo The Young Idea who had covered the Beatles *I get By with a Little Help from my Friends*. It was well produced by Tony Palmer at EMI and I managed to get the boys a slot on Top of the Pops before the record hit the Top 20. Alas, it did not go on to be a Top 10 hit, but it cemented a strong relationship between Ian and me that lead to him inviting me to join him and others in establishing Warner Bros Records as an independent label in the UK in 1969.

What an exciting time it was in the record business! At that time Decca and EMI were the majors and effectively controlled the business. Following along was Pye Records owned by ATV, one of the first commercial TV stations. Warner Bros product, including Reprise Records which was originally owned by Frank Sinatra, was licensed to Pye who had great success with 7" singles but was not strong on album sales, which was where the money was!

When we took the catalogue over from Pye, there were lots of great albums to market. These included Neil Young and Crazy Horse, The Grateful Dead, Randy Newman, Peter, Paul and Mary, and many more. Most of these were only available as imports from the USA at a very high mark-up. So we got to work to release this valuable back-catalogue plus the new albums scheduled from Burbank. These included a second album from James Taylor, the first having been released on Apple Records. Peter Asher, who managed and produced James's recordings, was frantically finishing this second album *Sweet Baby James*. We wanted to re-introduce James to the UK media, so we purchased 200 copies of the Apple album and mailed them to DJs, radio producers and journalists with a note announcing that JT's next album would be for Warner Bros but his Apple album was just to remind them of James's unique sound. It went down really well and when it came to promoting *Sweet Baby James* for Warner Bros UK, the job was really easy. He achieved maximum airplay on BBC Radio 1 followed by personal appearances on BBC TV including a superb 'In Concert' produced by Stanley Dorfman for BBC 2.

This new style of record promotion swiftly eased Warner Bros albums into the UK charts and sales boomed. We did not forget 7" singles either, and had huge successes with Kenny Rogers *Ruby Don't Take Your Love to Town*, Norman Greenbaum's *Spirit in the Sky*, and the Doobie Bros *Listen to the Music*. The Kenny Rogers single sold close to 1m copies; unheard of in this day and age.

We were not liked by EMI and Decca where Sir Joseph Lockwood and Sir Edward Lewis had ruled the UK record scene for so long. They were the major shareholders in Phonographic Performance Ltd, a company that negotiated airplay time with the BBC. The old thinking that too much airplay would adversely affect record sales was rapidly being disproved by the younger, newer labels and the pirate radio stations Caroline and London.

The two vice-presidents Mo Ostin (Reprise Records) and Joe Smith (Warner Bros Records) in Burbank California were so pleased with our UK progress that they asked Ian Ralfini to send Des Brown (Head of Press) and me (Head of Promotion) to LA for two weeks to get to know the staff at HQ and to meet some of the stars.

Chapter 20

It was a strange way to get to LA. Once we had obtained our visas from the US Embassy we were to fly from Heathrow to JFK on Air India then change to Pan Am or TWA from JFK to LA. All employees of Warner Bros were encouraged to use Air India whenever they could due to the film maker having so much money in India from the movie business that they could not repatriate to the USA because of exchange control restrictions in the sub-continent. It was good fun, as usually we were automatically upgraded to Maharaja Class on the Air India part of the journey – Chicken Vindaloo at 35,000 feet was great!

After a 32-hour journey we should have been sleepy, but when we arrived in nighttime LA we were just so excited that it kept us wakeful. Warners had put us into the Continental Hyatt House on Sunset Boulevard with great views across the city. The hotel had been created by Gene Autry and had a swimming pool on the roof.

The next day we picked up a Ford Galaxy soft top to get around the city. The car was great and so too was the music station WABC (?) which was pushing the Linda Ronstadt single *Long, Long Time*. Driving along Sunset, roof down with FM radio playing. We were in heaven! Years later Peter Asher was to produce Linda for Warner Bros. But even when I had seen her perform live in a small club in New York as the 'Stone Pony' years earlier she struck me then as a real talent.

During our first week in LA we spent daytime hours at the Warners offices in Burbank, meeting staff who we only really knew on the 'phone. They were great and very welcoming. There were several events organised too. We were invited to Kenny Rogers's house for an evening party which was very nice. Kenny was truly grateful for all the work we had put in getting *Ruby* to No 1 in the UK charts. For the middle weekend of our two weeks in the States we were sent to Vegas as guests of Nancy Sinatra who was headlining at the Sands Hotel. We had a giant suite and she arranged for us to see Elvis Presley's show at the Federal Hotel. On the second night there we saw Nancy's show too, and afterwards she invited us round backstage. We were standing talking to her when David Frost appeared. He looked at me in amazement. "What the hell are you doing here?" he asked. Before I could reply, Nancy told him that we were her guests for the weekend and that we had helped *Boots* into the Top 10 in London. I guess he thought I was out of place!

My parents were staying with my Mum's sister Margot and her husband Bill in San Diego, on their way back from Vegas to the UK. Des and I decided to fly back to LA via San Diego and visit them. I wanted it to be a surprise, so had 'phoned them from Vegas making out that I was in London, having worked out the time difference of 8 hours.

We hired a car from San Diego airport and drove to Margo and Bill's house; they were not in. We guessed they were at the beach, not much of a chance of finding them so we decided to pass the time with a visit to Bahia California. Tijuana was a half an hour drive from San Diego. At the frontier we were advised to leave the car and walk across. More surprisingly, we were advised to cut our hair by the US border guards. Not that the Mexicans would not let us in, but that the US would not let us return with shoulder-length hair! Crazy, as most young people in LA had shoulder-length hair. We were not impressed with Tijuana and were pleased to return to US soil.

We drove back to Margo and Bill's house and rang the doorbell. My Dad answered the door and I thought he was going to have a heart attack. He kept saying "You sod, You sod". He could not believe his eyes! Having got over the shock we were royally welcomed and taken out to dinner at a lobster restaurant on the quay side. It was great to see them but it just a flying visit as we had to be back at Warners in Burbank the following morning.

Chapter 21

Back in the UK there were many releases to deal with, also a James Taylor tour to organise. James was to tour with Carole King and the backing group Jo Mama; they wanted to play concert halls and smaller venues. I could have used one of the regular promoters like John Smith, Harvey Goldsmith or Barry Dickens, but I felt I could do it equally well myself. The costs could be shared between Warners and Carole King's Ode label via A & M Records.

I got on the phone and had very little trouble in booking the Royal Festival Hall London, Royal Exchange Manchester, City Hall Newcastle, and Fairfield Hall Croydon. The tour was a massive success and James's and Carole's current albums were in the Top 5 in the UK. Great timing!

At this time (1972) Deborah was pregnant again but her waters broke early and she was flat on her back in the Princess Louise Hospital in Hammersmith. Ian, being a great boss, told me to go home and look after two-year-old Sophie until the new baby was born. Deborah was in hospital for six weeks until George was born on 15th April weighing only 3lbs. I was warned by the consultant that he might not survive: difficult to believe today when he is himself married with three children and is a shareholder of one of the largest PR companies in London.

During this period and the time leading up to it, Elliot Roberts had been in and out of London making tour arrangements for Joni Mitchell, Neil Young and others. I had lunch with him in the Kosher Restaurant beneath the Warners office in New Oxford Street. He told me that he and David Geffen were setting up their own label, Asylum Records, to be funded by the Warners' group. He hinted that he and David were looking for someone to run it in Europe and would I be interested. Well, of course I was!

Elliot told me it would take some time and that David would be in touch with me a little nearer the date. It was to prove a huge disappointment to me in the end and caused me a fair amount of anxiety at home where I was looking after two-year-old Sophie and taking her to visit Deborah in hospital each day. I kept waiting for the phone to ring or a letter to arrive. It didn't happen so I started calling David Geffen in LA. He didn't take my calls and when I did eventually reach him, he told me that Atlantic would be their US distributer but that he had done a huge deal with EMI for the rest of the world. Only David could do such a deal for a label funded by Warner Communications but distributed outside the USA by rival EMI. I guess his very close relationship with Ahmet Ertegun enabled him to do what he liked. This was bad news for me because EMI had insisted on their own label manager for Asylum in London.

Deborah returned home from hospital on 17th April, but little George had to remain for a further six weeks while he grew and put on weight. It was a really difficult time for Deborah, Sophie and for me but a great day when we brought him home.

Chapter 22

Back to work again. Warner label VP Joe Smith wanted to bring his wife Donny to London on the crest of all the successes, so I had to think up a unique way of greeting them. I had bought an ex-London RT Bus as a promotion vehicle (RT1553) and retained a red livery. I got onto the printers who did our side panels and had 'There's only one Joe Smith' put on the bus sides. I arranged with our limo driver Dennis that he would follow me as a back-up just in case the police objected to the bus being parked on double yellow lines opposite Terminal 3 Arrivals. I picked up the RT from New Cross bus garage where we kept it and drove to our caterer Peter's place where we loaded up with champagne and nibbles; Dennis then followed me at a careful pace to the airport.

Fortunately, Joe's flight was on time and we had little trouble with the parking wardens: They didn't know what to do with a London double Decker bus parked on double yellow lines!

Our photographer was also there and captured the look on Joe's face when they appeared through the exit; it was quite something! Drinks on board, then Mr and Mrs Smith took the limo' to the Connaught Hotel. He loved the stunt and it helped me to make a very good impression with him.

Joe and Ian called me into a private meeting in Ian's office a few days later, the labels: Warners, Atlantic and Elektra were to get more independence within the WEA set-up in the UK. Joe wanted me to be 'his' man in London, Ian agreed with this and I was delighted. A new office within the WEA building for me and I was to furnish it! Off to Casa Pupo for a real Mexican feel. I was on top of the world! It was, however, not to last. Mo Ostin, who was slightly senior to Joe, wanted greater independence for Warner and Reprise and unknown to me had contracted Larry Yaskell, who had just been fired by A&M, to be my boss. Joe Smith was embarrassed and truly upset, but there was nothing to be done. I would not work to Larry!

It so happened that on the very same day I got the news of Yaskell's appointment, I was having lunch with Rod Stewart's manager Billy Gaff and his sidekick Mike Gill. We met at the Gallery Rendezvous in Beak Street, owned by my good friend Mr Yang. Billy and Mike noticed my glum mood, so I told them what had happened. Billy asked me if I would like to work with them setting up GM Records, to be funded by Warners for the USA/Canada and Phonogram (Holland) for the rest of the world. I was in no mood to remain with Warners as I felt stabbed in the back, so I said yes.

This all happened in the run up to the MIDEM Music Festival in Cannes in 1973, where I was due to make a Warners presentation. Billy and Mike also thought it would be a good platform on which to launch GM Records. This would all require some clever footwork!

Cannes in the last week in January was always a glorious escape from winter. The sun was shining, flowers were blooming and expense was usually not an issue. I was staying in the Port at the end of La Croisette where the hotel was owned by Forte, and that was where the Warner's presentation was to be made. Billy and Mike were at the Martinez where the bar rarely closed before 5am. I had also bumped into John Burgess from Air London who said that George Martin was hosting a dinner to which they would like me to come. I had known George through my days at Noel Gay Music where we published *Right Said Fred* a huge hit for Bernard Cribbins produced by George before his Beatles' days. I also knew John Burgess well as he was the producer of Peter and Gordon, having taken over from Normal Newell at EMI.

I had a painful meeting with my boss and dear friend Ian Ralfini who headed up WEA in the UK. He fully understood why I didn't want to work to Larry Yaskell but said he was very sorry I was leaving the company. The four years at WEA had been the most enjoyable of my time in the music business. Ian said that I was not really leaving as Joe Smith was delighted, I would be involved in their investment in Billy Gaff's GM Records.

The Warners part of the WEA presentation went really well and at the end Ian told the staff that I was leaving to join GM Records. He said I would be truly missed and praised all the promotional work I had done mentioning James Taylor, Carly Simon, Neil Young, Norman Greenbaum's *Spirit in the Sky* and Kenny Roger's *Ruby Don't Take Your Love to Town*. All achieving Top 5 successes aided by me and my team. Following this I was due in the Midem Theatre for a press reception to announce the launch of GM Records and my appointment as Managing Director. Mike Gill was a wiz with the trade and national press (UK and USA) and we got maximum coverage. This was useful as I had yet to negotiate the deals with Warners in Burbank and Phonogram in London and I had also to negotiate my salary package!

Chapter 23

Back to London to tidy up and close down my Warners office at WEA. Larry Yaskell was taking offices for the label in Greek Street, just off Soho Square. It was also rumoured that my long-term colleague Des Brown was going to join him as General Manager of Warner/Reprise!

GM's new offices were to be over the Marquee Club in Wardour Street, a building owned by the Marquee's boss Harold Pendleton. A fair bit of work needed doing, so we could arrange the accommodation to suit us. I fancied a large open-plan area with a big table around which we could all work. A couple of private offices too for when anyone needed to make a confidential call or meeting.

As far as staff, we needed sales expertise and I thought Alan Wade would be ideal. Alan had been sales manager for WEA in the Midlands and was good at pushing singles with the dealers. On the radio and TV promotion front we would probably use Phil Swerne or Ollie Smallman on individual projects. We could do all the groundwork from the office as I had a really strong mailing list.

Billy already had a core of artists ready to record, these included Ronnie Lane (ex Small Faces), Chris Jagger (brother of Mick), John Baldry, and Leslie Duncan, married to Jimmy Duncan, who was head of A & R for GM.

Billy Gaff and Mike Gill wanted a huge launch party at the Ritz on Piccadilly, but first we needed to plan a release schedule and make sure that our UK distributor Phonogram could slot us in. The next thing for me to do was to firm up the label's deals with Warners in Burbank for North America and Phonogram in London for UK and Rest of the World. We had no money in the bank so the first instalment of the Warners' advance of $250,000 was needed immediately.

Billy and I decided to make for LA as soon as possible. Mike Gill wanted to organise a Hollywood US launch for GM, so maybe we could get Warners to cover the cost!

Over the next few months we managed to get everything organised. The Warners deal was signed for an initial $¼ million and the Phonogram deal was set at 12 albums per annum at £12K per album. Things were looking good. Billy and I had new Jaguars and Mike had his debts settled. What we now needed were hits, and that was to be the difficult part!

I thought Ronnie Lane's *The Poacher* was most likely to score for us, after all he had a long track record with the Small Faces and he had given us a strong single and album. Chris Jagger sadly was recognised as Mick's brother rather than talent in his own right.

Alan Wade had established a good relationship with our UK distributor Phonogram so we set release dates for several singles to be followed by albums in Europe.

Releases in the USA were trickier to handle, and I had a sneaking suspicion that Joe Smith had done the deal so as to cement his relationship with Rod Stewart (who was managed by Billy) rather than enthusiasm for GM's artistes' rosta.

The Ritz launch party was very well attended and partially successful, although certain behaviour set the Ritz to ban any future music business events. It was expensive too at over £8000, which was a lot of money in those days.

We were certainly in the headlines due mainly to Billy and Mikes' close relationship with *The Express*'s pop journalist David Wigg. David was a really kind person who I had first met through TV producer Mike Mansfield whose agent I was for a short while when I ran Noel Gay Artistes.

Having started off so well with the management of GM; the large table around which we all worked and debated plans seemed to work, I was beginning to notice that certain decisions were being made outside of the office and without any input from me as Managing Director. Many of these decisions involved expenditure and I was put under a lot of pressure to collect more advance payments from Warners and Phonogram, made more difficult by GM's lack of chart success. This was a sad moment for me as I really enjoyed working with Billy, Mike, Alan and Andy Heath who ran the music publishing bit of Billy's empire.

I was still really friendly with my old boss Ian Ralfini who was still at WEA. We met frequently and he became my shoulder to cry on! He realised that I was becoming more and more frustrated at GM and that my time there was limited.

Ian was very friendly with Dick Asher the UK MD of CBS Records, and told me that Dick might call me: he was looking for someone to head up CBS's music publishing in the UK as Bob Britten, who had signed Gilbert O'Sullivan to the company, was looking to leave.

I had a call from Dick inviting me to lunch. He came straight to the point immediately offering me a three-year contract at twice my GM salary. Initially I turned him down as I didn't want to be disloyal to Billy Gaff and GM Records. But things became more and more difficult at GM: although we worked very hard to break singles, we had no success. The last instalment of the Warners' advance had been paid, the Phonogram money was still due but only on delivery of the next album which we could not afford to finish. Billy called a meeting at his flat, we were all to take a bank loan for GM, to be guaranteed against our homes. This was the final straw for me. I made an excuse to leave the meeting for ten minutes, telephoned Dick Asher and accepted his offer. I called my old friend and solicitor Ted Oldman and asked him to extricate me from my contract with GM – difficult times indeed.

Chapter 24

During my time at GM I had bought another old bus. Following in the wake of RT 1553 the Warners bus, I bought a former London Country single decker GS10. My dear and long departed friend Prince Marshall who established the London Bus Preservation Group's Cobham Museum, told me to go for GS 10 as it was the best of a bunch to be auctioned by LT's Chiswick works where it had been a staff bus for a few years. I offered £400 plus VAT prior to auction and my offer was accepted. I duly went to Chiswick and drove away my GS; it was the best way to be a bus driver – in your own bus!

I had some GM posters put on the bus which I intended to have driven round London, visiting Radio 1, Capital Radio, BBC TV Centre, etc. Ronnie Lane was playing at a venue near Hampton Court, so I put some refreshments on board the GS and drove it there. The gig was really good and the live performance of his single *The Poacher* went down a storm. Drinks on the bus went down really well and, guess what, Ronnie wanted to buy it to travel in. I suggested that there were a further two GSs for sale and arranged for him to visit Chiswick Works and choose one. He did and converted it into a travelling home for his ongoing tour.

Chapter 25

Back to reality, I had to tell Billy I was leaving GM, I did, and to this day he has never forgiven me. I have not seen him since 1973 but our mutual friend Mike Mansfield continually reminded me of Billy's anger.

I left GM on the Friday and started with CBS/April Music on the following Monday. Dick Asher had not been altogether open with me when he said that Bob Britten wanted to quit April Music. In fact Bob, Ivan Chandler and Brian Gibson, the existing staff at the 1 Wardour Street offices, had no idea they were to get a new boss, let alone be forced out of a job. My move on that first day felt a bit like 'out of the frying pan and into the fire'. Along with the three male employees were three young women, Barbara, Sue and Cathy. They seemed okay about having a new boss. They were fed up with the male 'pub' culture associated with Bob, Ivan and Brian.

I decided to interview each of the staff individually. Bob was first and he made it clear that he would not be willing to report to me. He was an angry man and I felt that Dick had not been totally straight with him. A few days later Bob reached an agreement and left the company immediately. Ivan and Brian were different and wanted to stick around.

April Music's offices were at 1 Wardour Street – on the 5th floor and no lift! It did mean, however, that I had independence from Dick Asher and the CBS staff who were located in offices on High Holborn, about a mile away. Also a mile away was March Artistes run by an energetic young agent Dave Woods. I don't think he was ever taken seriously by CBS and knew that Dick's ambition was to close it down.

Dick was keen for the publishing arm to be more closely integrated into the record company, so I was invited to attend CBS's A & R meetings each Monday evening in Dick's office. Also present were Dan Loggins Head of A & R, an American, Paul Russell a solicitor and head of business/legal affairs, Maurice (Obie) Oberstein head of manufacturing – a rather unpleasant middle-aged gay man who intensely disliked Dick Asher, and me, an unknown quantity who had been appointed solely by Dick at an inflated salary.

These Monday evenings were a total nightmare, a sort of private repetitive show where Dick, scotch and soda in hand, pontificated and name-dropped; Dan Loggins spoke New York music business jargon no one could understand; Obie was openly negative about any of Dick and Dans' ideas, Paul Russell who raised every legal problem he could think of, and me, the new kid on the block. A meeting that should be an hour to an hour half maximum dragged on for between 3 and 4 hours. I later learned that Dick liked to escape from the clutches of his wife Sheila whenever possible, so Monday nights offered a legitimate excuse. Dick was not a difficult or unkind man. He was an American lawyer desperately wanting to be creative. He was also a very impatient man who had been in the US Marines. His favourite phrase was 'Either shit or get off the pot'.

In truth, I found life as a music publisher lacked the front-line excitement of the record company as it was somehow always one step behind. I was a promotion man at heart, and in publishing I was expected to take a back seat. The salary was good but I was restricted to one of the big Fords, having previously driven Jaguars.

I had joined CBS/April Music in 1973 and by 1976 was getting really bored with the whole group. Dick had moved April Music to a new building in Soho Square. The record division occupied the upper floors and April Music the ground floor. And with this change bang went any feeling of independence.

There had also been movements at the US HQ of our parent company Columbia Records. Clive Davis, the boss of Columbia Records had left and Walter Yetnikoff, Dick's boss in CBS International, stepped into Clive's shoes and Dick was to be recalled to New York to take over Walter's old job. They had also sent Norman Stollman, to look after HQ's interests in London. Maurice Oberstein had, after a long fight, been appointed MD of CBS UK to replace Dick. Norman had a special task to keep tabs on Obie and to oversee my activities at April Music. We disliked each other from the start and my radar told me that I might have to move on soon.

I asked for a private meeting with Dick Asher to see whether he might give me a job in New York; he made all the right noises but I knew he had no intention of easing my career path.

Stollman was starting to put pressure on me. He was a detail man and wanted a better deal on sheet music which was looked after for us by Music Sales. He was sure we should get an extra 1p per copy sold. This and other minor irritants finally broke me one Monday morning, so I tendered my resignation to Obie. By 12 noon I had been ordered to clear my desk of personal belongings under the watchful eye of a security guard. I was then escorted from the building – it was true, this really did happen in US owned companies!

Chapter 26

What to do now? I had a little capital so a bit of time to find something new. I got a 'phone call from Tony Calder (TC) who had been Andrew Oldham's business partner in the early days of *The Rolling Stones*. He had gone into business with the younger Patrick Meehan and they were looking for someone to co-ordinate their activities. Both Tony and Patrick had reputations but they were fun and it might be a good temporary job. They, with Vic Lewis, had taken over the NEMS agency and record labels which were originally established by *The Beatles'* manager the late Brian Epstein. The offices were at Hill Street Mayfair and I agreed a monthly consultancy fee which would cover our mortgage and living expenses.

I enjoyed working with TC who had enormous energy and drive. To him the music business was fun. We looked at fixing up a record shop in Edgware Road to sell imported albums and cut outs from UK companies. TC was well connected in this area and stock was not a problem. TC was also involved in buying, modernising and selling expensive West End houses. I had no idea where the cash to do all this came from. For the first three months all went well. We were very busy and my monthly pay cheque was regularly cleared. Then month four came along and things started to fall apart. I was sitting as a JP at Southwark Juvenile Court in Camberwell when, during a recess, the 'phone in the retiring room went: it was for me from Bernie Lovewell, Manager at Barclays to say that my NEMS cheque had bounced. I went in to the office later that afternoon and TC said it was a glitch and that I should represent the cheque in two days' time. I did, and it bounced again. I knew then that I needed to get a proper job, so started looking right away.

I remembered seeing an advert in Music Week for a General Manager for Trojan/B&C Records. The owner of the labels, which had been bought out of receivership, was Marcel Rodd who also owned Saga Records and a pressing plant in North Kensington. Marcel had a reputation as a tough negotiator and of being a difficult man to work for. In spite of this, I knew that beggars can't be choosers, so I called him. No, he said, he had not been able to appoint a GM, was I really interested. He suggested that I came in to see him and to meet the accountant Bill who was currently running the day-to-day business.

The Saga building was a grim looking place at the very top of Ladbroke Grove, backing onto the Grand Union Canal. It was a true factory, grimy and dark. Marcel's office was furnished with cast-off chairs and a desk. He had advertised the job at 10K per annum but he and Bill tried to screw me down to £8K. I stuck to my guns and £10K was agreed. Marcel had a contract to hand and I signed up immediately.

The Trojan offices were on the top floor of the warehouse building and the entrance door was somewhat fortified. I asked Bill why this was and he told me that there were some disputes with former Trojan and B & C bands and artistes: they had not received any royalties since the labels were rescued from administration. A few of the artistes were very angry about this and had made threats to Marcel Rodd, hence the security measures. What had I got myself into? My first task was to look at the back-catalogue and see what we might press up and re-release.

I discovered that Clive had been running the labels on a temporary basis. Marcel Rodd seemed to dislike Clive so I wondered why he had employed him. Clive was resentful that I had been brought in over his head. It seemed the CBS situation repeating itself! He was sulking and spending lots of time away from the office so Bill told Marcel to fire him. The difficulty was that Clive had signed Rula Lenska to the label and there was a single ready to release. Rula liked Clive and would be very difficult to work with if he departed. The single came out and received some airplay but was not a chart success. Clive left and Rula's contract for one single expired.

My first visitors at Trojan were Bevan and Euton from the band Matumbi. Matumbi had had a minor chart hit with their single *The Man in Me* but this had been released over the period when the label went into receivership, so it had not received effective promotion.

They hated Marcel Rodd and were very angry with me. I thought they were good people under their anger and I promised to help them put Matumbi back on a strong career path. The band was one of the best reggae outfits in the UK and its members were hugely talented. Bevan, along with his brother Glaister, were the outstanding lead vocalists; Dennis Bovell was as always a great guitarist, writer and arrange; Webster was on keyboards; Eton Jah Blake on bass guitar; Euton on percussion and Bunny…on drums. More on Matumbi later as I would become their business manager on leaving Trojan. Other artistes were Dandy Livingston, Big Youth, and John Holt.

One day I had a visit from Bill Farley who I knew from his days as an engineer at Regent Sound in Denmark Street (Tin Pan Alley) when I ran Noel Gay. Bill was engineer on the Rolling Stones first recordings. He had signed Winston Francis and was producing a couple of singles. Now he wanted to do a deal with Trojan. Bill and I hit it off straight away and he already knew Dennis Bovell.

If I was to stay with Trojan beyond the three months' probationary period, I had to deliver something meaningful. I was friendly with John Blyton (nephew of Enid Blyton) who looked after musical copyrights for London Weekend Television and they were about to produce a network children's series *Fun Food Factory* for which there was a theme tune and musical content. Brian Forbes and his wife were involved. I talked to John and arranged a meeting with Marcel and Bill, the outcome of which was a contract between LWT and Marcel to release the theme from the TV show. This pleased Marcel no end and seemed to offer him some legitimacy in the business. I knew it was never going to be a cash generator.

In the middle of all this I received a call from Ron White at EMI Music Publishing. He was looking for a CEO for the London company which was now run from New York; would I be interested? I told him that it was early days for me at Trojan and that I did not want to get a reputation for jumping ship.

In parallel to this, my dear grandmother had fallen in the Fulham flat where she lived alone and had broken her hip. Against her wishes she underwent an operation in Charing Cross Hospital to repair the hip. This was successful but she got pneumonia and within a week she died. I was devastated. I had sat with her the night she died and held her hand, knowing in my heart that she would not survive. She was in her 91st year but I could not face the fact, when it happened, that she had gone. It still troubles me to this day that I was not with her when she died, on her own, in a hospital bed.

On the afternoon following her funeral I made my way to EMI Music in Charing Cross Road to meet Ron White. The new American boss was totally overbearing and I realised I could never work for him. I cut the interview short saying that I had to return to my family following the funeral; I said I would think about the offer and let Ron know the next day.

I frequently ponder where my career would have led if I had accepted the EMI job. The American only lasted three months, so I could have ended up running it world-wide. Had my Grandmother not died when she did and had I been more realistic about Marcel Rodd's empire then perhaps I would have taken the job.

Back at Trojan the Monday following the funeral I knew that my time at Trojan was coming to an end. Marcel was constantly chasing me for success but frankly he was not prepared to put any money behind the bands, and instead just wanted to milk the old back-catalogue.

Bill called me to his office and said that Marcel wanted me to resign. I refused and made sure that I was in the office from 10-6 each working day; happy to do my job. In the end

Bill persuaded Marcel to give me three months' money and I left immediately.

Chapter 27

After their earlier hostility me as a representative of Trojan, mere months later, Matumbi asked me to become their manager. I said I would become their Business Manager as my days of travelling to gigs was over. They agreed and we drew up a contract. EMI Records head of A & R Nick Mobbs wanted to sign the band so I went into negotiations with him and Martin Haxby and we struck a deal. This gave the band an advance plus recording costs to make an album; Roger Ames was to be their A & R manager. Roger thought highly of Dennis Bovell but did not really rate the band, a fact that was to become an obstacle in the future. I introduced band members to Bernie Lovewell at Barclays and a Matumbi account was established. They were legit at last!

With my new role as Manager of Matumbi, I needed an office. I had my pay-off cheque from Marcell Rodd but needed to create some longer-term income. I talked to my accountant Mike Henshaw who lived and worked in a lovely house on Regents Park East, owned by the Crown Estates. I was never quite sure whether Mike was a squatter or whether he paid just a minimal short-tenancy rent. Anyway, he had a spare room in the basement and offered it to me at a knock down price. I took him up on it straight away.

Bill Farley and Dennis Bovell had agreed to work together and wanted their own recording studio. They asked me to become a partner and find some cash; Bill had located some used equipment including a desk and a 16 track Ampex tape machine. He thought that £30K would do the trick. During my time at April Music I had become friendly with a car dealer from Essex, Tony Levoi. He was a really nice and enthusiastic businessman and was desperate to get into the music business.

Bill had found a basement in Berry Street off Goswell Road at a reasonable rent. I went to Tony and he agreed to put up the money for a 50% share; Bill, Dennis and me to have the remaining 50%. Ted Oldman put the legal document together and we were in business. Soon the basement was kitted out and Dennis and Bill began work.

One of the first tracks produced by Dennis was Janet Kays' *Silly Games*. It was co-written by Dennis and John Myatt and sounded like an immediate hit. We needed a label to distribute and promote the record but the big boys were not interested. I had become very friendly with the owners of independent distributors Lightning Records. They had taken quite a bit of stock from me during my time at Trojan. Alan Davision was my main contact. The business was owned by him, Ray Laren and Keith Yershon. I took Janet's single to Alan, who loved it but he didn't have a label deal. So I went to Rob Dickens at WEA and he agreed to a distribution deal with Lightning as long as we took care of the promotion. He also agreed to a £50K advance and that the Lightning label would trade as Laser Records. Alan was chuffed; Janet, Dennis and John were delighted and it was good PR for Berry Street Studios.

Alan and Ray Laren were keen to own a part of Berry Street Studios, which needed some more cash to upgrade the equipment. Tony Levoi, our current partner was not up for putting more money in, so Lightning Records bought him out. Once again I felt disloyal, this time to Tony, but we desperately need the new equipment.

I then thought about a publishing deal for Laser and after a few 'phone calls I ended up talking to Bruno Kretzschmar at Intersong Music, a division of Chappells. Bruno had worked for me at April Music and since my departure from there had made rapid progress through the ranks, becoming General Manager at Intersong Music on the departure of Ronnie Beck. I should mention that Bruno was my brother-in-law and was married to Deborah's younger sister Ursula (Modge) Main.

I managed to negotiate a further £30K advance for Alan on a 50/50 co-publishing deal with Intersong: not bad for a first go! I also had an agreement with Alan for a 15% fee of £7.5K: a useful contribution to my venture as an independent operator. This together with a 10% fee of £5K for the WEA deal would see me over the next few months.

Alan was also in need of an office away from Lightning, so I fixed for him to share my basement room in Mike Henshaw's house. Once Alan received the advances from WEA and Intersong, I put in my invoice for £12.5K. He refused to pay it, saying that we never had any agreement and that I had done my work as a friend. This was the beginning of the end for Alan and me. I should have got it in writing before finalising the deals. Alan left the office in Mike Henshaw's house, taking with him everything including the light pendants and owing a chunk of rent. Never do business with friends!

Luckily, I had in fact become a business advisor to Lightning and they agreed to pay me as a consultant. So that, with my small salary from Berry Street Studios, made my life financially stable again for the first time since leaving CBS/April Music.

Chapter 28

Things progressed quite well for a while, but without Alan Davison's involvement in Lightning Records, Ray Laren and his colleagues were losing interest in the creative side of our partnership. Ray found a buyer for Berry Street Studios and Bill, Dennis and I found a new sleeping partner willing to fund a new studio. Bill had found a basement in Emerson Street SE1, just round the corner from the Globe Theatre site, so we got cracking and within eight weeks Studio 80 was ready to roll.

Our new landlord Paul Keen was a nice person and his ground floor business was promotional gifts and nick-knacks. He was a bit stage struck too and liked telling his friends that pop stars recorded in his basement. We did have a few stars including Bob Geldoff, who had a rather unsatisfactory deal with Philips/Polygram who wanted to get him off the label. Through Dennis Bovell we also had the pioneer of African Beat music Fela Kuti and his band for a month. They brought wives, children, cooking pots and stoves. It was a strange time but the music was great.

Video was also just becoming big business and Bill had access to some good gear from the Commonwealth Institute who had just closed their TV studio off Russell Square. Our investor agreed on purchase so we had a mixing console, three cameras and a time-base corrector. The set-up looked good, but was never to get going.

Chapter 29

Just as the prospects of one venture began to fade, yet another opportunity emerged. Out of the blue, I received a phone call from movie director Gavrik Losely's PA. I got to know Gavrik when Dennis was commissioned to write and produce the soundtrack music for a low budget UK movie called Babylon. I negotiated the deal for Dennis who produced some great sounds, but Gavrik and I fell out on several occasions due to Dennis's poor timekeeping. I would frequently have an enraged Gav on the 'phone late at night demanding to know where my artiste was as he should be at the editing suite and was nowhere to be found. Fortunately, I had a rider in Dennis's contracts stating that the Manager (me) was not responsible for timekeeping and no shows, a clause I also had in Matumbi's contracts!

This time Gavrick's PA sounded me out on who might be good to head up a Music Company owned by Steven Bentink, the Baron as he was known in the business. Steven was a rich young man wanting to make his mark in the entertainment business and, according to Gav, had attracted just the wrong sort of managers to spend his fortune! I thought about this request and said I would call her back within the hour, which I did suggesting that I might be just the right person. She invited me to come and meet the Baron.

16 Bloomfield Terrace was the address, just round the corner from two of my favourite restaurants Le Poule au Pot and Hunan Chinese. To my surprise, I discovered that the man unsuccessfully running the Baron's music division was none other than Bob Britton who I had fired and replaced at CBS/April Music a few years earlier. It is cruel the way fate repeats itself!

Steven was very personable and totally under Gavrik's influence; very quickly I had a deal which allowed me to continue my interest in Studio 80 and allied projects while working for Stephen.

I had an extraordinary and memorable meeting on my first day with a loud-mouthed American who had previously come between me and Matumbi, telling them that I was useless and not a real manager and that he could guarantee their chart success. I had had run ins with him on the 'phone but never met him. Now, there he was sitting in my new office telling me about this great reggae band who had a shit manager (me) and shit record label (EMI) and that he was going to change all that. I let him dig himself in deeper before pointing out that I was that shit manager and that EMI would never release Matumbi from their deal as they had big plans for the band. He couldn't believe the situation as he stormed out of the office!

The Baron's label had some promising talent but not a very good delivery mechanism. We needed a distribution deal and a sales promotion team. I thought of Alan Wade who had been involved with me at Billy Gaff's GM records and now had an independent sales force. I was putting some structure into the organisation with the hope of chart success, which is what Steven yearned for.

Chapter 30

I was now involved with a studio, management company, record label and music publishing company, surely one of these was going to make us rich? All that was missing was a record pressing plant and I had plans for this.

I had been looking at record manufacturing ever since working for Marcel Rodd, where his 7" Lened presses churned out high quality singles for him and for third parties. It seemed like a license to print money. The set-up costs were high but there were grants available if one went to a Regional Development Grant Area such as Consett in Co Durham. I knew the area quite well and soon managed to make contact with British Steel Enterprise (set up to encourage enterprise when the steel plant closed) and DIDA – the Derwentside Industrial Development Agency. They were all very keen but asked where the expertise to make discs would come from? I had done some research when putting together my outline business plan. RCA had recently closed their pressing plant in Sunderland, meaning that there was a pool of expertise on our doorstep.

Roy Matthews, formerly EMI's factory manager, had been advising me on plant and he knew Bert Morrell who had been senior engineer for RCA. I met Bert who was very keen to get back into the business. The package was coming together.

Led by Laurie Haveron of British Steel and John Hamilton of DIDA, the package took shape. The Swedish press manufacturer Toolex Alpha would put in four new fully automatic presses (2x7" and 2x12") on an advantageous leasing deal. Roy Matthews would locate and install with Bert's help the boiler and high and low-pressure steam units.

BSC Industry would make a grant of £20K, the Midland Bank would provide a facility of up to £80K under the DTI's Small Firms Loan Guarantee Scheme and I had to find £20K form other sources.

I had been in contact with Bernie Lovewell my tame Barclays Bank Manager and he was able to arrange a £20K facility for me to be guaranteed against my share of our Clapham House. I remember collecting the Barclays cheque from Bernie which I then took on the train to Newcastle and then in a taxi to Consett. There, on sight of the Barclays cheque, BSC handed over their £20K grant cheque, which I then took to the Midland Bank in Newcastle. I now had £120K to start the company, Standard Pressings would soon be in business.

I had reserved through English Industrial Estates Unit 14A on the Consett No1 Industrial site, a large empty shed awaiting fitting-out. Old desks and chairs from the British Steel plant were freely available, so I had an office of sorts. Once I had the 'phone fitted I would spend whole days up there chasing deliveries. I was desperate to get up and running as soon as possible.

During this time I stayed with the McKechnies in Stocksfield, a half hour drive away in Northumberland. Eileen McKechnie and Deborah had qualified as doctors together at Newcastle and their first three children were the same age as Sophie, George and Eleanor. Eileen was a local GP and Roger, who had trained at Proctor and Gamble, was a manager at crisp makers Tudor Food Products in Peterlee, a division of Smiths Crisps.

Roger and I spent the late evenings in Stocksfield drinking and talking. He was fed up with his job as Tudor Foods kept promoting people over his head even though he was highly successful. One evening when he was staying with us in London, Deborah and I suggested to him that he should set up his own business. He said he had no money and how the hell could he do this? The next day I put in a call to Laurie Haveron at BSC in Consett and John Hamilton at DIDA and soon Roger and his colleagues Keith Gill, Ray McGhee and

John Pike were to launch Derwent Valley Foods, makers of Phileas Fogg tortilla chips, and to change the UK snack food business out of recognition. Roger and his colleagues eventually sold the business to United Biscuits and became millionaires overnight.

Chapter 31

While all this was going on, we decided on a cheap family holiday in South West France. One morning I got an irate phone call from Gavrick in London. Steven was very upset with me for setting up a pressing plant without telling him. Maybe I should have, but it was not part of my deal with him and I had kept it quiet. The man from Swedish Toolex Alpha had dropped by the London office while I was away and Dorothy, Gav's new PA, had intercepted him and obtained all details of the plans for the new plant. She was a busybody and didn't like me, so she blew the whole thing up as some sort of conspiracy against Steven.

I flew back to London to sort things out and explained to Steven that it was a project I had been planning for years and not part of my new deal with him. He accepted this but I knew my time with him would soon draw to an end. He and I went to a small Indian restaurant off Kings Road in Chelsea. Half way through lunch he excused himself and went to the loo. The Steven who reappeared after 10 minutes was a different person, energetic and pleasant, quite a relief to me!

I flew back to the family holiday in France knowing I would have to reorganise my working life once again on returning to England.

Tony Stubbs, my Newcastle Midland Bank manager, was anxious for Standard Pressings to start manufacturing as soon as possible, so I was destined to spend a fair amount of time in Consett. The day the presses were delivered was very exciting: they were all wrapped in high gauge polythene sheeting. The Toolex commissioning engineers were due the following week. Roy Matthews and Bert Morrell worked hard to commission the boiler and the high and low-pressure steam supplies and soon we were ready for the presses to be installed. The metalwork was to be manufactured down south to begin with, until we could afford our own metal plant. We asked them to supply us with metal just to test the presses and we had a ton of vinyl delivered.

We made our first 12" pressing which I still have in a box somewhere. Using my old promotional skills, I persuaded BBC TV Look North to do a piece on their 6:30 pm programme. We also got a mention in the *Newcastle Journal*. I was travelling up and down between London and Newcastle two or three times a week and working very long days. We advertised in Music Week and sent out flyers to all the independent record labels; the initial reaction was reasonable and we soon had orders mounting up.

I checked the bank balance on a regular basis and it soon became apparent that I would need a greater facility due to the delay in getting started and having to pay wages for six people in the meantime. Tony Stubbs at the Midland in Newcastle was very supportive and we got an extended overdraft to cover this build-up period. We got production up and running and were soon operating two shifts a day. It was now essential to make our own metalwork as ordering and delivering via Red Star rail in Newcastle was seriously holding up progress. Roy Matthews was great and from his store of redundant plating equipment we were soon making our own stampers. This gave us better continuity of production and improved our delivery times. We also had to make sure our customers would pay us on time and Shirley Robson, our Consett Office Manager, was great at chasing up reluctant payers.

Chapter 32

With all my waking hours spent getting Standard Pressings up and working, I had neglected the Studio and Management companies. I decided to leave the operation of the plant to Bert Morrell and Shirley Robson for a few weeks and concentrate on building up our studio work, limiting visits north to once a week.

I also wanted to give all our interests a profile at MIDEM, the annual music business fair held in Cannes each January. I organised a small stand and arrived early to set things up. Financially we were living a bit hand to mouth, our studio customers paid fairly well on time but factory customers were not so good and I had wages for six people in Consett to pay each week along with raw material and energy costs. I did not realise that an announcement made at MIDEM by Sony and Philips would affect vinyl record production quite so soon.

CDs were coming and very quickly too. The major European record companies were gearing up to move over to CDs even though the reject rate from the new presses was around 70%. At first I thought it would be good for us when the majors reduced their vinyl capacity to make way for new plant, but this was a short-lived hope.

We then considered putting up a plan to British Steel Enterprise and DIDA to expand Standard Pressings to manufacture CDs. We would need massive finance and we were still a young unproven outfit, so it would be difficult to raise the cash. I thought of involving Steven Bentink but quickly dismissed the idea. I called Roy Matthews who thought it would be a good idea and suggested that we consult an expert in the field of industrial investment. I also contacted Alpha Toolex in Sweden who had supplied our conventional record presses. Everyone seemed keen but no one wanted to be the first in with us.

Back at the factory things were running well on the production front but badly on the payment front. We were getting really strapped for cash. I had to make sure the wages were paid each week but we also needed raw material and our suppliers were not keen to extend our credit. They did however do a deal with Elldis Transport in Consett to store vinyl at their depot to be drawn down on receiving a phone call from London. This solved the logistical problem of waiting two days for delivery.

Chapter 33

Consett was a booming area with new companies setting up on the No1 Estate each week, it was good news for the North East and a Royal Visit was planned. Unfortunately, Standard Pressings was not on the itinerary for HRH Prince Charles. Electrac and Derwent Valley Foods were however and there was a good turn out on the day. Prince Charles came on the Royal Train right into Consett – the track from the old steelworks days was still in place. Roger McKechnie and his fellow Phileas Fogg directors were presented to HRH while I lurked with the also-rans in the crowd. It seemed a great day for them. What I didn't know until many months later was as soon as the Prince left, the guests at Roger's factory, regional directors of Barclays Bank, had to decide whether to put Derwent Valley Foods into receivership as they were overtrading and unable to stay within their banking terms. It was only the involvement of 3i's that prevented this from happening. We were not the only ones with a problem!

As Standard Pressings plodded on with bigger and more onerous financial problems I decided that we had started too late to compete with established larger pressing plants who were now rapidly moving into CD production. It was time to face the reality of the situation and cut our losses. There was just one more chance, however, before we threw in the towel.

We had been pressing orders for Terry Scully…whose company Pinnacle Records had a huge hit with Frankie Goes to Hollywood's "Relax". On the outside it looked as if he was awash with cash and could usefully own all or part of a manufacturing facility. We had dinner and struck a verbal deal: he would buy 60% of Standard and provide funding to upgrade to CD production. I would get some of my personal investment of around £80K back and become solvent once again. I went home to Clapham in a buoyant mood to await written heads of agreement from Terry's lawyers.

A few days later this rescuing dream was just that. Terry's company had gone into receivership with huge debts. Why did he not tell me?

Christmas was approaching and I was sure that the Midland Bank would not carry on supporting us for much longer. I went up to Consett to wish Bert, Shirley and the staff a Happy Christmas, knowing it might be my last visit as Managing Director. I personally bought whisky for all the staff, though they were disappointed as they were looking forward to a bonus. In reality however, we could hardly afford the wages that week.

I travelled back to London and the family. The second week in January I received notice from the Midland Bank that they were putting Standard Pressings into receivership. Two days later two receivers arrived at the plant and took over, looking for a swift sale. The sad thing in these cases is that whilst the bank got most of its money back, the other creditors, including Roy Matthews, who had supported us over the year, got nothing. I had always kept our creditors informed of our situation and they were supportive right up to the end.

My dream was at an end and I really did not know how I was going to carry on supporting the family and our home. Not only had the Midland foreclosed on Standard Pressings but Barclays were now putting pressure on me to repay the initial £20K I had borrowed to get the factory going.

Chapter 34

One morning Roger McKechnie called me from Consett. He could not believe what he had heard on the Consett grape vine. He had talked to his directors who were prepared to buy the assets of Standard from the Midland Bank's receivers and start up again. He had also spoken to my father-in-law Tom Main and his Kuwaiti friend Hasan Hadeed: they would put up £10k between them.

Roger's generosity, along with that of the others, was very touching, but I knew that it was too late and that the mass requirement for old vinyl records was over; CDs were in! Despite my certainty on this, they thought I was depressed and disillusioned by my fate so far and couldn't see beyond my current problems. They went ahead and purchased the assets. As the current presses were leased from Sweden, Alpha Toolex took them back and Roy Matthews provided four old manual presses; he was still being supportive!

I was not allowed to be a director of the new company or to benefit from it in any way. Roger did however take me on as a sales consultant on a commission only basis and he appointed Alan Probyn, ex-Proctor and Gamble, as General Manager. Bert Morrell didn't want anything to do with me: he thought I was a shit and had let them all down. I felt bloody awful and never wanted to see Consett again. I had to get a proper job, but where and what?

My mother had been shopping in Brixton and noticed that the old Bon Marché department store building, derelict for ten years, was being refurbished by BAT Industries plc and Lambeth Council as an enterprise centre for local people wishing to start their own small businesses. In the window they were advertising for a General Manager at £14K per annum. She called me and I applied for the position straight away. £14K would cover our immediate needs as a family. I would also be able to act as a salesman for the reborn record factory in my own time.

To my amazement I was invited to interview at BAT Industries HQ in Victoria Street but there was a problem. The interviews were on a Saturday and clashed with our planned visit to the McKechnies in Northumberland where I was to be Tom McKechnie's Godfather and Deborah was to be Samantha's Godmother. I couldn't let Roger and Eileen down as they had been so supportive to me and they were our oldest friends. My CV must have impressed the interview panel as they agreed to reconvene a week later just to see me. The interview panel was chaired by Alleyne Reynolds, CEO of BAT Industries Small Businesses, and comprised Cllr Jo Sinclair from Lambeth Council and various managers from BAT. I was not sure how the interview went, but I remember they asked me why I would apply for such a low paid job. I didn't tell them about my current crisis but did say that I wanted a career change, which was true.

Later that afternoon, Alleyne phoned me and offered me the job. The only one who disagreed with the panel's choice was Jo Sinclair. I was completely gobsmacked: I had a job and would start on March 1st 1984.

Firstly I had to get to know those involved in the Brixton project. Ron Gibson had been employed as a Temp to sit in the old shop window of the Bon Marche store and answer any questions passers-by might have. Gibson was a nice man who was more than a little disappointed not to have secured my job. He accepted me with a good grace.

Then there were the directors of the BEC: Alleyne Reynolds (who was my direct boss) based at BAT Industries plc HQ at Windsor House in Victoria Street, Suzanne Fisher BATI public affairs (who was to become a long-lasting friend), Richard Henchley BATI Company Secretary, Peter Evans BATI, Richard Kemp manager of BATI's Liverpool project, Keith Lewis Lambeth's director of business support, and Cllr Jo Sinclair chair of Lambeth's Employment Committee – the person who voted against my appointment.

I spent days in February at Windsor House and at another managed workspace in Coldharbour Lane, Brixton where much of our soon to be used office equipment was stored. These workshops were managed by Donna York, a very driven and competent black woman who I was to employ, along with Ron Gibson, as my two deputy managers at the Bon Marche.

Although I was not paid until March, it was good to have an office and a structure back in my working life. I still had many loose ends to tie up regarding the failed record factory business; working in my spare time to create sales for the new owners and doubting it would ever work profitably. I told Bill Farley and Dennis Bovell that, due to the factory going bust, I would not be involved in Studio 80 on a day to day basis as I had to earn a living to pay school fees and the mortgage. I would, however, be around to advise in any helpful way.

Bill told me that he had stopped trading at the studio; the VAT people and the landlord had been chasing him and that the owners of the leased recording equipment had taken away the desk and 16 track tape machine. Bill too was looking for a new start!

Chapter 35

Alleyne Reynolds called me at Brixton to ask if I would man the stand at an employment-creation exhibition and conference in the crypt of St Paul's Cathedral in the City. He had been chosen by LENTA (London Enterprise Agency) to escort the guest of honour, Princess Alexandra, around the crypt. I put on my best suit, which I had worn for my successful interview at BAT and turned up at St Pauls.

This is where I met four men who were to become firm friends and colleagues over the next years: Brian Wright CEO of LENTA, John Hyatt London Director of Business in the Community, Barry Horner an official with the Employment Department, and Peter Brown GM of LENTA. John, Barry, Peter and I were to become the 'famous four' of employment creation in London.

Me with the Princess in the Crypt of St Paul's Cathedral in London

The exhibition was enjoyable and I was presented to Princess Alexandra: there is a photograph in the book to prove it! What an existence of contrasts in my life: the winding-up issues of Standard Pressings in the North East and the exciting world of Small Business creation in the South East. My experiences of a failing business were to stand me in good stead when advising others of the pitfalls awaiting all new entrepreneurs.

I kept in touch with Roger McKechnie and helped Alan Probyn as best I could to create business for the re-opened factory. It was then that I discovered Roger was to be awarded an MBE for his success with Phileas Fogg in Consett and that he and Eileen were coming to Buckingham Palace to receive the medal from the Queen. I was told they were celebrating afterwards by going to see the musical CATS, so I 'phoned my old school friend Peter Roberts who was a senior manager for Cameron MacIntosh and arranged a surprise champagne bar in the Green Room during the interval.

Meanwhile, I discovered that on the day in question I was summoned to an examination by the Official Receiver in Stockton on Tees to be questioned on my part in the downfall of the record factory. What an awful contrast!

Alleyne Reynolds had encouraged me to visit as many Small Business Centres as possible before the opening of Brixton, so I arranged to visit a project in Newcastle sponsored by the Burton clothing group; a legitimate reason to visit the North East. The night before my appearance in Stockton I stayed at the Holiday Inn in Middleborough, my dad's hometown. I didn't sleep very well wondering what was in store for me in Stockton the next day.

In any event, it was not too bad. I had drawn a very modest salary at Standard Pressings, always kept creditors up to date with our standing and just had to accept that we started too late in a market that was rapidly turning to the CD. I was asked to swear an affidavit confirming my views and I was free to leave. Waiting on Darlington station for the train to Kings Cross I felt relieved that this first step was over, although I was well aware that there were more problems to be dealt with in time. I also felt a little jealous that whilst I was being castigated by the Receiver for my company's failure, my best friend was receiving his MBE from the Queen for his successful business!

Back in London there was plenty to do in the months leading up to the official opening of the Bon Marché project – The Brixton Enterprise Centre.

Chapter 36

I had to get to know all the people I would be working with at BAT Industries plc and Lambeth Council, along with officials from the DoE. Alleyne Reynolds suggested that I use the hospitality dining rooms at Windsor House for this, using his name for bookings.

Ted Knight, Leader Lambeth Council, Rt Hon Patrick Jenkin SOS Environment, and me.

Ted Knight was leader of Lambeth Council. His reputation was well known and I was impressed by how he got things done. Looking back, I think opposition members and officials at Lambeth were truly scared of him.

Strangely, Ted and BAT Chairman Pat Sheehy seemed to get on, both being big hitters in their own worlds. They were also big men and able to silence a room when walking in. Pat Sheehy was committed to BAT's social programme, although he and Alleyne never got on, which could be a bit of a problem.

One afternoon I was the only person in the office on the 11th floor at Windsor House, BATI's Victoria Street HQ. There was an exhibition at the Royal Academy that BAT had sponsored, to which most of the senior and middle managers had gone. I heard a phone ring in the Personnel Director's office. It rang and rang, with no reply. Then a similar unanswered phone in Planning just rang and rang. Eventually the phone where I was rang, I picked it up. "Sheehy here, where the fuck is everybody and who are you?"

I explained to Mr Sheehy that I was the new boy employed to run Brixton. He told me to keep a strict eye on expenditure and I got the distinct impression that he didn't trust Alleyne to do just that. "Get him or somebody senior to contact me as soon as they get back, I've not been to the bloody exhibition yet and I'm the Chairman of this bloody organisation!" There and then I decided to gain Pat Sheehy's confidence – a move that was to stand me in good stead in the years to come.

The building work at Brixton was running to schedule and we decided on a launch date. This was to be delayed a bit due to the discovery of asbestos cladding round the old boiler in the basement.

The opening was held in the retail shop front with Frank Bruno as the guest of honour. Pat Sheehy, Ted Knight and Patrick Jenkin, Secretary of State for the Environment were present. They arrived early and Ted and Patrick were laughing and joking together; all very friendly. Then the press arrived with cameras, it was like turning on an electro magnet as the Leader of the Council and the Secretary of State shot apart and glared at each other. It immediately turned me into a political cynic!

I made a speech which was well received and Frank Bruno declared the project open. I always wondered whether my past might just catch up with me as I was highly visible in the local press; it never happened!

Chapter 37

My main job was to fill the building up with new small businesses as soon as possible. BAT were keen to generate income to part-payback their initial investment of some three million pounds. There was only one way to do this: through publicity and advertising. I was keen to let small businesses know that we were not just a landlord but offered a business support service too. A main switchboard with a memorable number was needed. I thought 274 4000 would be good so I took the BT local area manager to lunch in Trinity Gardens where an excellent restaurant had opened. We soon had the number confirmed. Now we needed a slogan, so I came up with "274 4000, can I help you?" I thought we should go on commercial radio with a slightly humorous advert featuring the above text but followed up with 'That's a nice little number!' We needed Kenneth Williams and I asked LBC to make the commercial which we would use on LBC and Capital Radio.

It was a great success, Kenneth was terrific and got it just right and the enquiries started coming in. Within the first eight months of the Centre being fully open we had built over 90% occupancy, unheard of at that time. We also became the place to visit, and the skeptics within BAT senior management started to support us and feel proud of what we were doing.

Tom Long, BAT Industries' finance director, sat next to Kenneth Clarke, who was a Minister of State in the Thatcher government, at some grand dinner hosted by BAT subsidiary Argos. Ken had heard of our Brixton success and wanted to visit. This was quickly arranged and he and Tom turned up one afternoon. Ken was really impressed and what I didn't know until much later was that he asked BAT to lend me to government to help create more projects like Brixton.

In the meantime poor Alleyne Reynolds, without whose drive and enthusiasm the project would never have seen the light of day, was hauled up before Gerald Dennis, Deputy Chairman of BAT and Chairman of Small Businesses, and fired for having overspent the construction budget by £1M! He was told that it was not the overspend but the fact that he didn't warn Pat Sheehy of the situation that got him fired. Without Alleyne's support I would never have been appointed Manager of Brixton, which saved my sanity and my family's well-being. I shall be ever grateful to this unique man.

One Friday evening, I received a 'phone call at home from Gerald Dennis. He told me that Alleyne's contract was not being renewed and he asked if I would take his place on the BAT Industries' Small Businesses Board. I couldn't believe my good fortune and accepted right away.

The following week I received a call from Norman Perry, a Grade 4 at the Employment Department, where Ken Clarke, along with Lord Young, headed up Thatcher's employment creation initiatives. He asked whether I would like to become Deputy Director of the Inner Cities Central Unit which he ran. He told me it was a full-time job and that Ken had written to Pat Sheehy to request my secondment.

I didn't want to quit Brixton or BAT so suggested to Norman that I split my working week 50/50 between BAT and the Central Unit. He did not like this idea so I asked him to allow me a week to try and resolve things. Another problem was that Pat Sheehy too said I would have to choose, that it would not be possible to do two jobs at once!

I went to talk to Heather Honour, Sheehy's speech writer and former civil servant. She was very helpful and together we put a note together to convince Pat that I could do both. After a few days he agreed, so now I just had Norman Perry to convince.

During the time when I sat as a magistrate in the Inner London Juvenile Courts one of my Chairmen was Lady Howe. She and I hit it off right from the start and she always said to ask if she could be of help in any way. I called her and explained my difficulty with Perry: I knew she and Geoffrey were close to Ken Clarke. She told me they were having dinner with the Clarkes that weekend and that she would put my case to him.

First thing on the following Monday Norman called me saying that I had powerful friends and that a 50/50 split of my time between BAT and the Inner Cities Unit was now fine by him! What a turn my career was taking. I could never have planned it that way.

The following day I got a message from HR at Windsor House to say that I was being promoted to Grade 14 which meant a rise from £14K per annum to £30K per annum. This salary was in line with a Grade 5 in the Civil Service. The good news was that I would retain this salary level at the end of my secondment on return to BAT where I was to become a full staff member with all the usual benefits: pension, car, medical insurance, the lot!

L-R Me, Ken Clarke QC MP, Tom Long FD of BAT Industries plc, and a Brixton tenant.

Chapter 38

Norman Perry's Inner Cities Central Unit was based at Steel House in Caxton Street, just round the corner from Windsor House and right opposite Caxton House where David Young and Ken Clarke ran the Employment Department.

Norman asked me round and showed me my new office, he told me that as a Grade 5, I would have a desk, conference table and that the carpet would go 'right to the wall'! I didn't believe at first that this was a real situation.

It was here that I met Monica Gordon, my PA who would be working with me for a good many years. Monica had worked in Norman Tebbitt's private office and really knew her way around the bureaucracy of government.

I was just getting used to working 2 ½ days in Caxton Street when a General Election was called. The Tories got back in and Lord Young and Ken Clarke were re-shuffled to the DTI. David Young was Secretary of State for Trade and Industry, sitting in the House of Lords. Ken Clarke was promoted to the Cabinet as Chancellor of the Duchy of Lancaster, Minister of State for Trade and Industry with a special remit for enterprise creation, sitting in the Commons. Ken had a special advisor, a young man called Jonathan Hill. He was Ken's gatekeeper and I quickly learned how to get things into Ken's Red Box: not through Private Office but through Jonathan Hill!

Lord Young sent shock waves through the old DTI. He and Ken summoned all Grade 5s and upwards to a presentation in the restaurant at 1 Victoria Street. It was more like a sales presentation in a commercial company, where Lord Young instructed everyone to go for it and shake off the old-style regulatory image of the DTI. Senior officials were not impressed.

My other 2 ½ days a week were spent looking after Brixton and other BAT Industries' employment creation projects in Liverpool, Southampton, Deptford, and Peckham. At Brixton it was becoming apparent that we needed a business advisory service to help our small business tenants grow their businesses. BAT, along with LEntA, Business in the Community and the London City Action Team put this idea together which I presented to Pat Sheehy, asking him to become Chairman. We were to call the Agency the South London Business Initiative – SLBI for short. I had enlisted the help of an elder statesman of the black business community in London, Dr Wally Baker. He had been a great support during the period of setting up the Brixton initiative. We advertised the post of Chief Executive for the SLBI in the *Times* and the *Voice*. Wally applied and was appointed. He was by far the most outstanding candidate.

L-R Norman Perry Grade 4, Ken Clarke and me Grade 5.

The supporters/shareholders of SLBI were BAT Industries plc, Freemans plc, British Rail, Lambeth Council, BITC, LEntA, and the London City Action Team, headed up by a young David Normington who went on to become Perm Sec at Education, then Home Office as Sir David Normington, and finally as Civil Service Commissioner and Commissioner for the Office for Public Appointments (OCPA).

One day Barry Horner and John Hyatt cornered me over a drink. They couldn't tell me what they knew but said not to be fazed if I was asked certain questions about myself which might appear curious. They hinted that my name had been put forward for an honour based on my work in South London. This never came to anything but the following year Wally Baker was awarded a well-deserved MBE in the New Year's Honours. My award had gone to someone else! Years later, over a drink, I asked Sir Robin Young, when he was Perm Sec at DTI, to check out what happened. His enquiries did show my name on a list, but the recommendation was never taken forward. Such a shame for me as my Dad received an MBE for his work with fringe theatre; it would have been great if we had received awards together!

One day I was up a ladder in our bedroom at Ferndale Road when my mobile rang. It was Richard Branson who had been nobbled by Lord Young and agreed to help create a Virgin-backed enterprise centre. We chatted about this and I suggested that he might have a few thousand square feet of unused space at Virgin which might be a temporary home for a few new small businesses. Richard seemed genuinely keen to help potential new entrepreneurs and we agreed to keep in touch. Before we rang off, I reminded him that we had met before when I had Althea and Donna on Top of the Pops with their number one hit 'Uptown Top Ranking'. Richard stole the act from under my nose by offering the girls a new recording deal and £100K advance! What he didn't take into account was that the real talent was Joe Gibb, the Jamaican producer of the record. The girls went on to record an album at George Martin's studio in the West Indies at enormous cost and they were never heard of again!

Chapter 39

I had not forgotten the re-launched record factory in Consett. In my spare time and usually with Alan Probyn the new GM, I had visited, 'phoned and generally badgered independent labels to use the plant. Unfortunately, the old manual presses did not produce the quality pressings we had made with the Alpha Toolex presses. This was not just due to the technology but the fact that we were using re-cycled vinyl.

One morning I got an urgent call from Roger McKechnie in Consett. He had closed the plant and put the factory into receivership. It had become obvious to him and his accountants that the business was insolvent, a situation he could not be associated with as it might go against Derwent Valley Foods' efforts to either sell their business or float on the stock market. It was a shock to me that it happened so suddenly, but not a surprise!

Johnny and Jean at Buckingham Palace

I asked Roger whether he had informed my supporters Tom Main and Hasan Hadeed, who he had just persuaded to inject more capital: he had not! No point in delaying, so I called them immediately. They were furious and deeply shocked with Roger and asked me why he couldn't have warned them instead of taking more of their money. I felt bad but I had warned all concerned that volume vinyl pressings were a dying item and that we should not try too hard to revive the business. (Shame the Consett Plant was not mothballed, as today there is a rising demand for 12" vinyl discs).

This was an uncomfortable period for me but it had a silver lining. I had entered the Brixton project into the City of London's Dragon Award's scheme, not thinking for a moment that we would stand a chance. One morning I got a call from Stephen O'Brien, CEO of Business in the Community, to tell me that we had won this prestigious award. I took my life in my hands and 'phoned Pat Sheehy's office direct. I explained the situation to his PA Sue Small and, after a few seconds, was put through to the man himself.

Pat was truly delighted. This was just the good news the Group needed. The award evening was a grand affair at the Mansion House to which Pat was invited as a guest of honour. He declined the offer, instead offering Deborah and I the chance of receiving the award in his place, which we did.

Deborah and me at Mansion House after receiving Dragon Award from Lord Mayor for Brixton project.

Chapter 40

My time as Number 2 in the Inner Cities Central Unit was very enjoyable. Time was spent visiting the 17 Task Forces and travelling with ministers on the Action for Cities Road Shows. I got to know Ken Clarke better and spent time with ministers from other departments too, including John Patten who was later to become Secretary of State for Education.

At the end of my first year's secondment Ken Clarke asked for me to stay for a further year. My split role between BAT and DTI worked very well as both HQs were a few hundred yards from each other in Victoria Street.

One amusing event I recall well. I was doing a BAT morning at Windsor House when Sue Small, Sir Pat Sheehy's secretary, asked me to pop down to see the Chairman. He had heard that Ken Clarke had received some sort of promotion as a member of the Cabinet. He asked me to draft a letter of congratulation to Ken, which I duly did. The next morning I arrived at my desk at the DTI to find an orange folder awaiting me. Inside was Pat's letter to Ken and scrawled across it was a request for me to draft a reply, so I wrote to myself! Somewhere today I still have copies of these two letters.

The Inner Cities Unit was now two years old and my boss Norman Perry was looking to his next move and promotion. He was a DoE man seconded to the DTI and this had not endeared him to his own Permanent Secretary Sir Terry Heiser whose loathing of the DTI was no secret. Unfortunately, this dislike had rubbed off on poor Norman, so a regional directorship in the West Midlands with DoE had become impossible. He lobbied Ken and Elizabeth Llewelwn-Smith, a Departmental Secretary at DTI and was finally offered the West Midlands RD for DTI: not such a big job as DoE.

Norman made it known to me that my term at DTI would be coming to an end and that Ken Clarke had another post in mind for me before I returned to BAT Industries as Director of Community Affairs in a year's time. He wanted me to take on responsibility for the inner-city work of English Estates, the wholly government-owned manager of many industrial sites in England. A new company was to be formed 'English Estates Inner Cities Ltd' and I was to be joint Managing Director! What a turnaround for me as EE had been my landlord on the Consett No.1 Industrial Estate where I had established and then failed with Standard Pressings. I was well known to the local EE management at Consett and would have to make sure that my past would not jeopardise my new position or my long-term future with BAT. I told Norman that I would be delighted to accept the job but needed a week to finally make the decision.

My main contact in Consett was now a senior manager with EE in the North East. I decided to go and see him in person.

I rang EE's HQ at Team Valley in Gateshead and was told that Graham was at a regional conference for two days at Craythorne Hall, a country hotel just south of Middlesborough on the A19. I booked myself on the next BMI flight to Teesside, picked up a hire car and made for the hotel.

I felt quite brazen and somewhat nervous, and when I arrived, I asked reception where the meetings were taking place. I was told that delegates were on their tea break in the hotel lounge, and on looking in I spotted Graham. He was somewhat surprised to see me but quickly assured me that my secret was truly safe with him. He said that I had had some bad luck but that was behind me as far as he was concerned, and he wished me good luck in my new post.

The next morning, I called Norman and confirmed my decision to take the job. By the time I got back to London a message was waiting for me from Tony Pender, Chief

Executive of EE; would I come to Gateshead for lunch to meet senior managers?!

Life had taken a strange turn and I needed to share my good news with others. Deborah had been kept in the picture all the way but outside of my close family no one knew. I phoned Roger McKechnie and jokingly told him that I might be becoming his landlord, although Consett was hardly an Inner-City area! He was totally amazed by my news. I then arranged the lunch at EE for the following week and agreed to stay with Roger and Eileen for two nights around my visit to Gateshead.

The old English Industrial Estates Team Valley HQ had a very austere feel about it. When I arrived, having driven down from Roger's house in Stocksfield, I was met by Tony Pender. He was a quiet refined man whose physical appearance of a rugby playing prize fighter belied his true personality. I was introduced to his second in command and henchman Peter Southern, who I took an instant dislike to. Tony and Peter played mister nice and mister nasty, and I was warned never to cross Peter.

I was treated like a VIP with lunch in the Board Room and I met most of the senior staff. Tony and Peter were very keen to find out just how close I was to Ken Clarke. They seemed to think that he was keen to get rid of EE through the privatisation route and if this were so they wanted a (big) piece of the cake.

My other half at EEIC was to be David Rhodes, a very nice, very tall man from Teesside. We were Joint Managing Directors; David was North and I was South. We hit it off straight away, eventually becoming close friends along with architect Tony Stringer.

Peter Southern gave me a budget for our new London office which was to be located in the Brixton Business Centre, the project I had developed for BAT Industries; good to keep it in the family.

During my first month at EEIC I quickly realised that David and I were to have very little power over inner city developments as Peter Southern firmly controlled the purse strings. Knowing this, I had to decide whether to engage Ken Clarke in a bloody battle to remove Peter Southern's influence or, in fact, to remove him completely from the organisation. I am ashamed to say that I opted for the quiet life knowing that I would be returning to the private sector in under one year. This meant that EEIC was just window dressing for the government's regeneration and employment creation initiatives, a totally impotent part of the organisation.

Chapter 41

The time was fast approaching for me to return to BAT Industries plc as Director of Community Affairs. I would be based at Group HQ at 50 Victoria Street and have a broad responsibility for the company's social conscience.

During my secondment to DTI, (Sir) Pat Sheehy, Chairman of BAT Industries plc had decided to switch the company's social responsibility focus from enterprise support to support for education. Kenneth Baker, the then Secretary of State for Education and Science, had been working with (Sir) Cyril Taylor to develop a business targeted style of secondary school to be called a City Technology College. He had approached Pat and asked BAT to become a major sponsor and Pat had responded positively by offering £2m towards establishing a City Technology College somewhere in the North of England.

My Dad Johnny Hutch MBE on my shoulders at Macmillan
College the then City Technology College in Middlesbrough

It was quite a co-incidence really as Middlesbrough, my
father's hometown, was chosen. The local authority was
really against the CTC idea as it effectively bypassed them,
being directly funded by central government. The war with
Middlesbrough council was to be fought for many years. A
site had been identified, a former Roman Catholic Girls
School on the Stockton Road, almost under the A19 viaduct.
Gerald Dennis, deputy chairman of BAT Industries, had been
nominated as chairman of governors and a senior former
Wiggins Teape man, John Chumrow, had been seconded to
manage the early days of the project. Other partners were to
be Sir John Hall of Newcastle's Metro Centre and two other
smaller industrial supporters.

John Chumrow had identified a local project manager in former newspaper publisher and military man Tim Willis, who was to become a firm friend and colleague during my initial years' involvement at the CTC. I was told to ease myself in gradually but was assured that eventually I would be BAT Industries main man on the Middlesbrough project.

Alexander Macmillan, Lord Stockton, had been invited to become a governor and he had been asked if the College could adopt his father's family name of Macmillan. Thus, Macmillan College, the Teesside CTC was created.

The school opened in 1989 with a year seven intake of 80 local children. It was three times over-subscribed and local parents loved it. The local authority hated it and forbade their local schools to have anything to do with Macmillan College on pain of instant dismissal of any staff doing so!

John Paddick, a former headteacher from the Midlands was appointed to run Macmillan College, he was a rather gaunt and driven man who was to prove an ideal first head teacher in this difficult environment.

My first few years as a governor of the college were really quite good as Ken Clarke had become Secretary of State for Education in the Thatcher government. I had kept in touch with him; we still had the occasional curry together and he was keen to hear about Macmillan's progress.

Gerald Dennis, the then Deputy Chairman of BAT Industries plc, was very firm in his support for Macmillan and the regular governors' meetings were very productive. Gerald was a no-nonsense chairman and very good at getting things done. This contrasted with his high position in BAT Industries where he and Pat Sheehy were not getting on, even though it was Gerald who had turned the single purpose tobacco company into a diverse conglomerate with international interests in financial services, retail and paper manufacturing. I never did find out how he blotted his copy book!

Chapter 42

The BAT Industries' board decided that support for education should be the focus of the company's community activities for the forthcoming years. Therefore, I was tasked with disposing of the employment creation projects in Brixton, Toxteth and Southampton and distancing the company from its involvement in the enterprise agencies. We had, after all, supported these Thatcher initiatives for a decade.

John Higgins, who ran the retail part of the Bon Marche project in Brixton, had made it clear he would be interested in taking over from us if we decided to exit. He already had a good relationship with Lambeth Council who were our original partners in the Brixton Small Business Centre based in the Bon Marche building. So the Brixton exit looked quite promising.

Toxteth was a different matter however, as the project had never washed its face financially, yet it provided a necessary support base for 100 plus small businesses in the old South Western Dock building in Liverpool. There was a very dedicated staff headed up by a scouser called John Jones; he was supported Sue who made sure John stuck to the rule book! Also on the Liverpool Board was Paula Ridley who was to go on to become Chair of the Victoria and Albert Museum in London. She had been on the board of the Tate Gallery in London and was Chair of the Liverpool Tate Gallery. Paula and I did not see eye to eye on many issues but we became firm friends and colleagues.

The project was run for most of its life from BAT Export in Woking where Tony Liddle, a really nice relaxed executive, allowed John Jones to run the initiative as if it was his own. This made my job particularly difficult in the run up to exiting Liverpool. This was not helped by the fact that I had worked with the former Liverpool Cigarette Factory Manager Dave Cheetham to sell off the buildings and land to the Merseyside Development Corporation for £1. Dave still has the cancelled cheque framed on his sitting room wall! There is a photograph somewhere of Barry Bramley handing over the key to the Liverpool factory to Michael Portillo, the then Environment Minister.

In disposing of the enterprise initiatives my main task was to protect the reputation of BAT Industries plc, then 8th in the FTSE Top 100 companies; publicity of the wrong sort could be price sensitive too!

In the end, we found a company that managed workspace to take over from us and to take on most of our staff. John Jones did not want to work for them, so I was able to give him a very generous severance package but it never made up for his loss of position locally. Dear John went off to do other things and sadly died a few years later.

Chapter 43

Being part of the Public Affairs team at BAT, although not an insider, I knew that something was afoot. Lots of closed doors and clusters of advisors. Eventually I was made an insider and learned that the company was to be demerged: tobacco would become a plc in its own right and financial services (Allied Dunbar, Eagle Star and Farmers in the USA) would merge with Zurich Insurance of Switzerland.

Simon Cairns (Lord Cairns) had taken over from Sir Patrick Sheehy when Pat retired and Simon asked me if I wanted to join him at Allied Zurich plc, the new 50% UK holding company for Allied Dunbar Assurance, Eagle Star Insurance and Farmers Insurance in the USA along with the Zurich Insurance businesses. The other 50% was to be owned by Zurich Allied AG based in Switzerland. He also said that he had another 'offer I couldn't refuse' if I was to join him at Allied Zurich plc following the demerger and merger!

It was 1997, and Princess Diana had died in the Paris car crash. Lord Cairns had been asked by Buckingham Palace to keep an eye on the very new Diana, Princess of Wales Memorial Fund which had been established by lawyer Antony Julius to handle the huge amounts of donations flooding into Kensington Palace in her memory. The fund was being run from three locations: Kensington Palace where her former staff were still in a state of shock; Comic Relief whose chief executive had been seconded-in short term; and Mishcon de Reya, the late Princess's solicitors. It was a nightmare scenario I was told. Apparently staff at the three locations disliked each other and the situation was totally out of control. Simon Cairns wanted to second me to the fund for 6 months to sort things out. If I agreed, then my future with Allied

Zurich plc would be assured at least until 2001 when I would be 60. I went home and told Deborah: it was a crazy situation but also quite a challenge. Next day I told Cairns I would do it!

With HRH PoW on royal visit to Hungary.

My first move was to meet the staff, so I arranged to visit Kensington Palace, KP, where the late Princess's staff still worked, in very privileged surroundings. I cleared the police control and was met by the Comptroller of Diana's household. He was very tense and still traumatised by events. He introduced me to other members of HRH's staff, including Paul Burrell, who were occupied in tidying up the offices and her residence in preparation for closure. They were very unhappy bunnies.

I was asked, in a fairly aggressive manner, what I was going to do to improve the situation. They also told me how dreadful the staff at Mishcons and Comic Relief were; they did not understand the depth of grief and sorrow caused to her personal staff since the tragedy in Paris. I kept an open mind. The KP staff were acting like spoilt children but they all were genuinely grief-stricken.

Next I went to meet the Chief Executive at Comic Relief. She was a genuinely nice person and a good charity professional. She was concerned that all donations received should be logged and properly treated. Many of the envelopes received at KP had included cash.

Then I went to Mishcons to meet Antony Julius. He had installed two PRs donated by Tim Bell, in the offices to handle the press. It was a nightmare job with the Red Tops breaking new stories every day. Simon Cairns wanted me to calm the PR situation down as a priority: frankly an impossible task. I went back to Windsor House and shut myself in my office. I had to come up with a plan to improve things quickly.

Chapter 44

My experience in the music promotion business was to come to my rescue. Whenever I had a difficulty getting airplay for singles and albums I always called in all involved staff to work together, round a large table in a War Room scenario. It's amazing how it can work and overcome the most difficult problems. Today it's called Teamworking and Sharing!

What the Diana Fund needed was four thousand square feet of open-plan office space in Central London with car parking and some second-hand furniture and office equipment.

The office equipment was not a problem as BAT Industries was about to demerge and Windsor House was full of desks, chairs and PCs, which were all going for scrap. I would, however, have to keep any donations from BAT a secret: 'Tobacco Company funds Diana charity' was not a headline I wanted to see in the Red Tops!

Premises were another matter, but I thought that a major property investor might just help. I knew that Legal and General owned Millbank Tower which had empty spaces and parking. I went to see the building manager at Millbank. He had been a huge fan of Diana and said he would speak to L & G's Head Office. I was unsure how successful he would be, or how long an answer would be in coming. Three hours later he called me to say that we could have three and a half thousand square feet of space free for a year, including three car parking spaces. I couldn't believe my luck. Simon Cairns couldn't believe it either and straight away arranged for me to meet Diana's sister, Lady Sarah McCorquodale, who was to chair the Fund.

All involved at a high level were very impressed with my success so far. This was good for me as what I had not known at the time was that the Charity Professionals involved with the Fund did not want some middle manager from industry in charge of a charity: they wanted some soft, wooden charity worker who was past it! Now they all felt I was the right choice!

Later that afternoon I called the three branches of the fund and invited them to come and inspect their new work environment. I then spoke to the building manager at BATCo and made arrangements for 20 desks and chairs to be delivered to Millbank Tower. I spoke to the IT manager and organised for 25 IBM computers with new software licenses to be delivered and installed.

BT were also pleased to help and I asked for an easy-to-remember telephone number and a small exchange on an ASAP basis. I had never known such willingness to help. The late Princess's name just opened doors so easily – more so than even the mention of Frank Sinatra in my Warner Bros days!

A week later I gathered all staff in our newly kitted-out offices and gave them a pep talk. I told them that they would be expected to work together and co-operate in pulling the fund into some workable form. I said that I would be there to help but that I insisted on proper professional conduct and behaviour. I stressed that I would like to get on well with everybody but that I would be tough if necessary. If they all ended up hating me then that was tough: in six months' time I would be back in my new day job as Corporate Affairs Director for Allied Zurich plc!

Chapter 45

I was splitting my days between BAT/Allied Zurich and the Diana Fund. Life was good and challenging. I got on very well with Simon Cairns which was a relief to me. He had been very cold towards me when we first met at BAT Industries after he had just taken over the chairmanship from Pat Sheehy. But now all seemed well as I was, I thought, a valued member of his personal staff.

I found myself organising events at William Kent House in the cause of establishing the Allied Zurich brand. The Belcea String Quartet provided concert evenings in the music room of the historic house. It was an excellent venue and I was able to invite my VIP contacts including David Normington, then Permanent Secretary at Education, Dame Rennie Fritchie the Public Appointments Commissioner, Ken Clarke and David Blunkett.

Following a very successful AGM organised by me and my team, I approached Simon Cairns for a pay rise. I had discovered that my opposite number in the Zurich operating company was being paid £110K per annum; I was on 81K pa. I did a note for Simon in the hope that he would support my claim. I was keen to maximise my earnings to eventually enhance my pension. I knew that once the share structure of Allied Zurich plc (London) and Zurich Allied AG (Zurich) were unified, I would be redundant and asked to retire.

Simon called me in and told me he would not support my promotion request and that if I was unhappy with that he would not discourage me from resigning. I was furious and felt personally rejected, but I decided to stay as I enjoyed my job so much. Simon's refusal to support my ambition was history repeating itself as I had asked my previous boss at

BAT (a long-term colleague and friend) to support my request for promotion to Grade 16, a step that would have made a huge difference to salary, share-options and general benefits at Windsor House. I had asked him to do this just prior to my transferring from BAT to Zurich: he refused too! Turned down by two old Etonians in a three-year period. As an outsider, you can't rely on the old boys from 'Slough Comprehensive'!

The workload at Allied Zurich was decreasing as we approached the inevitable unification of the London and Zurich listed shares. Lord Cairns was to be seen less and less as he too was looking for a job post Allied Zurich as a chairman in a FTSE 100 company: something that eventually eluded him.

Simon was also involved with the Commonwealth Business Council and CBC was to organise an event in Melbourne alongside the 2001 Commonwealth Heads of Government Conference. The boss of the CBC was a lifelong international official Mohan Kaul who had been appointed during the launch of CBC at the Commonwealth Heads of Government Conference in Edinburgh in 1997. Simon Cairns was CBC's first chairman.

As my workload decreased at AZ, Simon asked if I would like a secondment to the CBC to help organise a business conference alongside the Heads of Government meeting in Melbourne. It would mean a month in Australia where I had never visited before. I spoke to Deborah and she said I should accept. I was concerned too because my mother was due to undergo a minor operation at St George's Hospital during my time away. I mentioned this to her and my dad and they both insisted I should go and that she, Mum, would be just fine.

Having agreed this with Simon Cairns I set about organising my trip.

My main contact at CBC was to be Gregor MacKinnon, a really nice Canadian man. He and I were to spend quite a lot of time together during 2001 trying to organise a good conference in Melbourne. What I hadn't taken into account were the prima-donna personalities involved!

Simon Cairns as CBC Chairman was fairly laid back and this left a vacuum in which certain aggressive and self-opinionated board members threw their weight about. One particular Australian was quite challenging and he was on his home ground in Melbourne. Also, Simon and Mohan Kaul were not arriving until the last minute: not a comfortable scenario!

The Australian member had also insisted on us employing his favourite PR lady whose inexperience was to prove a major irritant and burden to Gregor and me during the build-up to the conference. We suspected there was a strong relationship between them which set her up as an immovable obstacle!

Our timetable was three weeks in Australia to set up and organise arrangements, then following a period back in the UK, to relocate to Melbourne for three weeks around the Commonwealth Heads of Government Conference.

The first three days were taken up travelling between Australian cities, so two days in Sydney, two days in Canberra meeting federal officials, then off to Queensland to meet officials there. All extremely nice people but with much rivalry between Australian States to deal with.

I grew to like Melbourne better than the other cities. It was very cosmopolitan with plenty of spicy food available which I inflicted on Gregor and Mohan. It was strange for me as I assumed Mohan, who originated from Malaysia, would like spicy food. In fact, he didn't and much preferred traditional English 'public school' fare!

We finally put the finishing touches to the Business Forum Programme and headed back to the UK. Little did we realise that 9/11 would intervene and all our hard work would be lost in the resulting cancellation of all international business events.

Still commuting from Winchester to London each day, I was sitting in Café Quattro at Waterloo Station when I was approached by Patrick Wintour who was a member of Prince Charles' inner circle. We had often chatted over coffee in the early mornings; Patrick's Office was over the café. He told me that he might have something of interest to me?

It was 2001, and celebrations were about to take place on the 10th anniversary of Nelson Mandela's release from prison. As much of the work for equal rights in South Africa had taken place in London there were to be great celebrations here. And they were looking for an experienced person to help coordinate the month-long event. The plan was to close off Trafalgar Square and create a concert venue for South African music and entertainment, the climax of which would be an appearance by the great man himself. Patrick said he would like to put my name forward for the job!

What an opportunity of a lifetime and incidentally an opportunity to work with organising committee member actor/author/painter Sir Tony Sher, a close friend of my father Johnny Hutch MBE. Dad had worked with Tony and his partner, RSC Director Greg Doran on the production of Tamborlaine the Great at the Barbican in London, training Tony to climb a rope, turn upside down and slide back to the stage whilst delivering his lines!

I told Patrick that I should love to be involved, especially as Deborah and I had previously met Mandela during one of his private visits to London when we had taken him, along with others, to a theatre in the Strand to see a South African musical. A magical moment when, during the interval, the audience started to applaud, and Mandela went up on stage and spoke without notes for half an hour to a rapturous ovation.

L - R: Nelson Mandela, me & Deborah at South Africa House.

Chapter 46

Back in the UK I was still commuting from Southampton to Waterloo every day as Deborah's job was located at the Royal South Hants Hospital in Southampton.

To ease my travelling life I decided to travel 1st Class on South West Trains, expensive (£75K over 14 years!) but worth it in increasing my quality of life. Little did I know that this extra expense would also lead to several worthwhile contacts and work.

I regularly caught the 0657 train from Southampton to Waterloo, and it was in the 1st class carriage that I first met Paul Pedrick. He was a larger-than-life former RN Petty Officer who had served in the Falklands where he kept the helicopters flying. He now worked for Railtrack plc, the then rail infrastructure company controlling the UK rail network. He was approachable and very friendly and enjoyed a good joke or two. Just the person to cheer me up on cold, dark early mornings. The Railtrack people all travelled together on this train, picking up others at Southampton Airport Parkway and Eastleigh. At the airport another Railtrack man joined the train, another Paul – Paul Worthington who I soon learned was Deputy Company Secretary of Railtrack. Both Pauls were very engaging and Worthington, a former RN officer, was an excellent foil to Pedrick's jokes.

A while later on, when the Government put Railtrack into liquidation, Worthington employed me to help structure a rescue plan for all the current and former employees of the company who had put their complete life savings into the purchase of Railtrack plc shares under the Employee Share Option Scheme, which then became worthless on liquidation. The rescue scheme was never implemented as the shares were eventually allowed to regain some value, so shareholders got some money back.

The friendship with the two Pauls and their wives meant regular meetings at Chinese, Indian and Thai restaurants in Southampton. Paul and Carol Pedrick even spent time at our flat in Spain, close to Gibraltar, where Paul had spent time in the Navy. I remember well Pedrick turning up on Southampton Central Station platform 1 with a hairnet on his head! This was a result of him getting hooked on 'Hairnet' brandy (the bottles have net wrapped around them), our main tipple for late evening drinking in Spain from where Paul and Carol had just returned.

As previously mentioned Paul Worthington had become interested in the not-for-profit work I undertook. This was to lead to me advising Railtrack on the setting up of a hardship fund for individual shareholders who lost their savings and, in some cases, their homes through investing in Railtrack shares, the price of which crashed when the Government suspended the company from trading on the stock market. Most employees had bought at the top of the market when the price was around £18; it subsequently crashed to under £3.

Chapter 47

It is now March 2020 and much has changed since I last wrote my journal, having retired from Zurich Financial Services in 2000. During my latter working years I had acted as an Independent Assessor for the Commissioner for Public (Ministerial) Appointments, OCPA as it was known. It was an enjoyable activity although not very well paid. I worked across six government departments, DTI, DCMS, Home Office, and several NDPBs (Non-Departmental-Public-Bodies). Interesting work of checks and balances, making sure appointments were made on merit and trying to stop ministers' shoe-horning unworthy favourites in to powerful positions.

Sadly, for me, this all came to an end around 2010, when the Cameron Government, on the recommendation of my old friend and OCPA Commissioner Sir David Normington, dispensed with our services overnight! So much for transparent oversight!

Since retiring from both my day job and then OCPA, I had kept busy with two pro-bono roles: Chair of UK Trustees for IFAW (International Fund for Animal Welfare) and board member of The Diana Princess of Wales Memorial Fund Ltd. I had continued to commute daily from Winchester to London as Deborah's job continued in Southampton until 2012. She had been diagnosed with breast cancer in 2005, had a mastectomy and was on tamoxifen. The treatment had been challenging but successful during the early years, but on retiring and moving back to the London house she discovered that the cancer had spread. Her care moved to the Royal Marsden Hospital Chelsea where she was treated until her sudden death on December 2nd 2015. All those years of hard work, saving for a retirement she was never to enjoy.

In early 2017 my old travelling companion Paul Pedrick died quite suddenly having been in hospital for investigations, and early 2020 Sir Patrick Sheehy died, I guess it's that time of life!

On a brighter note, my elder daughter Sophie, a senior health correspondent at the BBC, took the brave decision to become a solo mum. Margot Rebba Violet Hutchinson was born on 18th December, 2018 at the Chelsea and Westminster Hospital and is the most beautiful addition to the family. It is a great sadness to us that Deborah, who supported Sophie so much in the decision to have a baby, is not with us to enjoy this precious child!

My middle child, my son George, his wife Milly and their three children, Molly (17), Clara (15) and Tom (12) live in Herne Hill. George is a very successful corporate adviser on risk and reputation and works for some of the world's leading corporates and NGOs. Milly is also very successful and runs the communication department in the UK and Ireland for a leading international company. George is also a great cook and Milly loves the guitar and singing and between them the kids play the base, electric guitar and the drums. They have a lot of friends and family around, but who would want to be their neighbours?

My younger daughter Eleanor, an anthropologist at the London School of Hygene and Tropical Medicine, her husband Ned and the two boys, Finbarr and Wilfred moved from Geneva to Dun Laoghaire. Six months later I was delighted when they decided to return to London to a little house, a 'home for heroes' that Ellie found in 2005 when she was writing up her PhD. They are lucky enough to have one of the best state schools in the country at the bottom of their road and her bright little boys will go to school there when they are old enough.

So life without Deborah goes on. During the run up to her sudden death in December 2015 we had talked quite frankly about my life without her. She told me that the first year would be tough but that the second anniversary of her impending death might be much tougher. As usual, she was quite right, and now on the run up to my nearly five years as a widower I am beginning to see the faint rays of recovery.

Since her death I have travelled a lot between London, Geneva, Dun Laoghaire Co Dublin, Trie sur Baise in the Lot, my small now recently sold apartment at Torreguadiaro/Sotogrande in Spain, and my Northumberland friends in Corbridge and Hexham. I feel that my feet have hardly touched the ground.

I have found solace in poetry writing and have put together a book of Deborah verse to be called, *Good Grief*. It is the best way for me to express my deep feelings of loss to those dear friends and family who have looked after me in this now strange new world.

GOOD GRIEF

An extract from *Good Grief*, a selection of poems/prose in celebration of Deborah Hutchinson's life, to be published at a later date. In memory of Deborah 1943–2015.

When your partner of many years dies
Your very private love affair becomes very public
You have to share her with the many family and friends
Who also loved her
This can be touching
But also challenging
As the intimacy between you has vanished
Because she is no longer there
To share with you the glances and the knowing looks
That were the strengths, the foundations
Of that bond that the two of you shared

Now lost…forever.

WATCHING

I sit here in the hospital day unit
As you sleep
Whilst the blood transfusion
Re-energises your failing system.

I cannot believe this is happening to you
The one I love so dearly
My partner for a lifetime
No magic wand in hand
How long have You got
I do not know.

Now......I know.

HOW DO I DEAL WITH THAT

I just remember the smell of her hair
How do I deal with that
The touch of her skin
So smooth and cool
How do I deal with that.

Now she's gone
No more to see
Just lodging in my memory
Still that hollow empty feeling
Leaving my emotions reeling

Life goes on
And on..........

OH HOW I MISS YOU

Oh how I miss you
And the wind still blows
Oh how I miss you
And the rose still grows

It was never meant to end like this
But I had no resurrection kiss
To bring you rushing back to me
In full health and fancy free

Oh how I miss you
And the wind still blows
Oh how I miss you
And the rose still grows

You fought the illness as only you
With your inner strength could do so true
But in the end your medic crew
Ran out of answers forcing you
To abandon your fight to survive
And I know now you're not alive

Oh how I miss you
And the wind still blows
Oh how I miss you
And the rose still grows

THE SPACE YOU LEFT BEHIND

I'm filling the space that was left when you died
I sleep on your bed
I sit in your chair
I talk to your friends
I drive in your car
I try to remember
When I last saw you.......
.......Was it December?

In familiar places silent weeping
Though normality's back a-creeping
Into all those nooks and crannies
Life's still quite raw
Not like before........you died!

FEET DON'T HIT THE GROUND

Now I'm done in Dunleary (Dun Loghaire)
En route to those cheery
Dinners near Auch
Well you know how it goes
Then from Toulouse to Paree (Paris)
Well I know it's not me
Am I running away
'Cos I dare not to say
I'm still missing you badly
On my own now so sadly

Will my feet hit the ground?

My good family and friends
Try to make their amends
And I love them most dearly
For keeping me cheery
When it's you that I'm missin'

Your cheek now so cool
Am I just an old fool
Trying to remember
That old September
Song whose lyrics show
When I'm tearful I go
Travelling more to the places
Where we went with embraces

Will my feet hit the ground
Ever............?

GLIMPSES OF DEBORAH -
"OUT OF THE CORNER OF MY EYE"
(Inspired by W H Mearns "Yesterday Upon the Stair")

Out of the corner of my eye
Was it you I did espy?
But when I looked
You were not there
I'd like to think I did not care

But since you died
These half-glances
Make me feel
That there are chances
Just to catch what's nearly there
Like a haunted little prayer

Maybe it's a forth dimension
Memories of you when there is tension
When my thoughts are full of worry
Or in too much of a hurry
These blurry images swiftly flee
I pray you are not scared of me!